Every Step Is A Gift

F.R. "Fritz" Nordengren

Every Step Is a Gift
F.R."Fritz" Nordengren

Copyright © 2015 F.R. "Fritz" Nordengren
All rights reserved. No part of this book may be reproduced in any form by any means without the express permission of the authors. This includes reprints, excerpts, photocopying, recording, or any future means of reproducing text.

Cover photo of the author at Faro de Cabo Finisterre, the lighthouse at Cape Finisterre.
Photo courtesy of Sandra Rott,
used by permission

Published in the United States by Two Mile Ranch
ISBN-13: 978-0-9903241-4-0
ISBN-10: 0-9903241-4-1

Every Step is a Gift

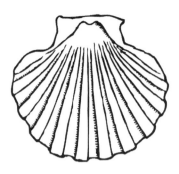

Preface

There is a photograph of a lone hiker standing at the side of a narrow road in fog and mist so thick, it looks like special effects rendered by a computer program. But the dampness on the hiker's shirt, the slight bit of fog on his eyeglasses, and the sweat in his hair prove the mist and fog are quite real. The lighting suggests it is midday. His backpack is decorated with flag patches from more than a dozen countries. The hiker, a man in his fifties, is looking into the lens. He has a half smile, and the look in his blue eyes and on his face suggest he is not lost but rather that he is looking for something or someone.

That photograph is of me at the beginning of my pilgrimage across Spain. I would show it to you, but being honest, I've never seen it. It was taken by strangers, a couple from Israel who were recently married and hiking the same pilgrimage for their honeymoon. I gave them a small card with my name and an e-mail address they could use to send the photo to the photo-sharing website Flickr.com. It was one of several dozen cards I gave to strangers and new friends during my forty-day walk. The couple was resting when I met them. After the photo, we shared our goodbyes, and I walked on.

If this had been any of my other travels, I would have taken photos myself. You'll read more about that later. Instead, I wrote a letter each day to my three children in hopes of sharing the experience of my pilgrimage across Spain with them and offering insight to life that I—as a father—might share with them.

Mentally, I had been preparing for this day for about a year. My pilgrimage is officially named the Camino de Santiago de Compostela, or the Way of Saint James. It's often nicknamed the Way. The Camino pilgrimage is walked by believers to the cathedral where the remains, called *relics*, of Saint James are buried. Saint James is James the Greater, one of the Twelve Apostles of Jesus. There are a few different routes to Santiago, Spain, and I chose the most popular and the most traditional: the Camino Frances—the French Way. Of the two hundred thousand or so pilgrims who arrive in Santiago each year, one hundred thousand walk the Camino Frances. So while I felt as if I were walking alone, I told my children before I left that I was "walking with my hundred thousand closest friends." However, I didn't know any of those friends yet.

What is the Camino? For centuries, pilgrims, authors, philosophers, and spiritual leaders have tried to define the Camino pilgrimage. What many agree on is that the pilgrimage is a metaphor for life, that the mental, physical, topographic, and spiritual adventure portrays a life. It's a sort of experiential theater. You'll read more about that later, too, but between the guidebook, some Internet postings, and some other travel over my life, I had a general idea of the mental rigors of being separated and in a country where I had few native language skills.

Physically, I had all I needed for the day. A CamelBak filled with water rested in my backpack. If you don't know, it's a water bag with a connected drinking tube. This was the first time I'd used one, and from the beginning, I liked its convenience. I had a sandwich. Not just any sandwich, but a sandwich made from a real French baguette. It was wrapped in paper and tucked in the cargo pocket of my pants. The cargo pants were old and a bit worn. They stay on a hanger at the back of my closet between long trips. I wore them first when my twin teenagers were born. Now, they fit snugly around the waist, and the pockets have tiny holes. But they have plenty of life left.

Even at the altitude, I was warm enough without a jacket, and wearing one would trap my body heat and drench me in sweat. But the cool mist had me drenched anyway. My head was putting off enough heat that it fogged my eyeglasses.

After meeting the honeymoon couple and having the photo taken, I tucked the glasses away in the other cargo pocket of my pants. Since I couldn't truly see much, I was guiding my walk by what I heard in the distance and what I could make out when I got close to see it. I had a guidebook with a pictogram map of the route and a few landmarks noted, along with a sheet of paper with first-day directions given to me by a volunteer in the French office for pilgrims. There are two places on the route that have very specific instructions and accompanying photos. The guidebook said the high point of today's walk would be 1,450 meters, or roughly 4,750 feet. The photos I've seen taken on clear days show an expansive view of Spain and France. I showed those photos to my wife before I left.

She asked, "How many days will it take you to cross the mountains?"

"That's just the first day," was my answer.

What I share in the next pages are the letters I wrote my children at the end of that first day, and the remainder of the forty letters I wrote during my pilgrimage.

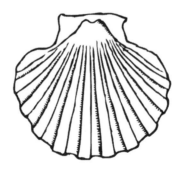

Day One:

"Invite yourself along"

Roncesvalles, September 20

Dear Chase, Noah, and Cara,

My day began in clear weather in the small town at the base of the Pyrenees Mountains where I spent the night. The French town of Saint-Jean-Pied-de-Port rests near the border with Spain. The sun was beginning to rise to my left as I walked down the narrow stone street that runs between the town's two historic gates: the Porte Notre Dame and the Porte D'Espagne. The small shops were still closed, and as it became bright enough to see, other hikers switched off their headlamps as we crossed the river bridge and looked for the sign that pointed to the Route Napoleon.

Yes, that Napoleon. He had used this route to get his troops in and out of Spain during the Peninsular Wars in the early 1800s. I could only imagine, and hope, that my backpack and gear were lighter than the kits used by his soldiers.

The Route Napoleon is well known for its beauty. And also for its challenge.

"Longest and most arduous," said a guidebook.

"Strenuous."

"One of the more demanding walks."

And like all things adventurous, I am not sure if the reviewers were bragging or complaining.

In the walk's early hours, we pilgrims were spaced out along the road in pairs and trios. Some hikers would pass me briskly, and I would pass others. As we climbed higher, the farmsteads hemmed by tidy fences were replaced by groves of trees that filtered the sunlight. By midmorning, Napoleon's route was obscured by thick, white mist, and it felt as if I were walking alone.

The weird part was when I began to hear metal clangs. First one clang, then another. Another closer, another farther away. The clangs continued for many minutes before I realized they were cowbells coming from both down the slope on my right and above me on the left. They made a rhythmless and random pattern. When I finally saw through the fog, the bells were on sheep. In this mist, the bell's purpose was necessary. A flock could have been easily lost from its shepherd.

I was walking with my hundred thousand closest friends

I stopped in the road for a moment to consider my situation. I'd flown halfway around the world, and now I was crossing a mountain nearly a mile high. Behind me or ahead of me were the hikers I began the day with in Saint Jean. Other than a honeymoon couple and another solo hiker with a yellow flower on her green backpack, I was walking alone in the fog. The thought crossed my mind that I was the one who needed the cowbell.

Faith defies logic, and I had come to the border between France and Spain for a walk of faith. And now, alone, unable to see father than I could throw the guidebook in my pocket, and having the very French instruction sheet warning me not to get lost or take the wrong turn, I accepted this first day as a demonstration of faith. I turned off the roadway and up a rocky path. Oddly, the cowbells encouraged me: I had come here to walk, and I was not turning back.

It is the twentieth day of September 2013. Today's destination, on the other side of these mountains, was the town of Roncevaux. That's the name used by the French, and it's painted on a small sign pointing the way. In Spain, the town is called Roncesvalles.

My walk out of the mist and the Pyrenees led to a twisty path and road recommended by the volunteer staff in the pilgrim office in Saint Jean. It cut back and forth across a few trails and fields before reaching the town limits of Roncesvalles. Ahead of me was the former monastery mentioned in Hemingway's *The Sun Also Rises*. Hemingway's characters, Jake and Bill, took the bus past the monastery in Roncesvalles on their way to Burguete to catch trout in the river.

It's there I took a shower and spent the night. Along the Camino, there are hostels for pilgrims called *albergues*. There are scores of them on the Camino routes. The albergue in Roncesvalles is modernly renovated with new bunk beds and storage lockers, making it look more like an IKEA furniture showroom than a monastery.

By late afternoon, the sun was shining and pilgrims were drying clothes, airing out ponchos, and taking showers to shake the first day's hike off their bodies. For nearly everyone, it is the first or second night in an albergue. We were still learning the ropes, and most of us still had a set of clean clothes. Folks who had packed too much or had extra items to share had left them on a table marked *FREE*. It looked like a rummage sale at a camping store. Everyone was sharing stories of hiking over the Pyrenees.

There is no ceremony at the border joining France and Spain, no passport stamp, no full body scan, no long lines of travelers. There is a public drinking fountain where I refilled my water. After walking alone most of the day, a fellow pilgrim surprised me as he walked out of the mist and joined me at the fountain a few moments later. We exchanged the customary Spanish pilgrim greeting of *"Buen Camino."*

The pilgrim looked at both of our wet clothes, hair, and faces, and then he offered one word before he walked on: "Baptism."

I finished filling my CamelBak with water and followed his path in the mist a few moments later, reflecting on his defining word. The idea to walk the Camino had come to me over a year ago. In the metaphor of life, today was my baptism.

Remember how I used to say I was walking with "a hundred thousand of my closest friends"? I began to meet them by inviting myself along. After settling in at the albergue and doing a bit of laundry, I ran into John, John, and Peter. I had met them and their wives the previous night in Saint Jean. I had introduced myself to John, and he explained that he had organized the pilgrimage for a trio of couples. They were all from Canada but had spent time in Iowa. When we were in Saint Jean, I invited myself along as they were headed off to find a beer. Well, that's not true. As they later explained, they were off to find "a religious bookstore." But we were clearly sitting in a tavern with icy cold French beer in front of us when they said this. They told me that on one of their prior trips, some of their companions didn't approve of alcohol, so "look for the religious bookstore" became a code for beer. Now in Roncesvalles, we swapped a few tales about the mist, the fog, and the long climb up and down the mountain.

Outside the albergue, I introduced myself to Dave and Pam, also from Canada. I asked them to take and post a photo of me to the Flickr account. It was probably the first photo you saw. I invited myself along as they made reservations for dinner—a necessity at some of the restaurants on the Camino, I am told. At dinner, the background noise and table size made it hard to have conversations with more than one or two people away, but I met a few others: Kevin from Chicago was at the far end, with Dave and Pam between us. A woman from the UK who lived in Barcelona recently was opposite me, but I didn't hear her name. On my right was Sandra, a German woman whose husband had walked the Camino two years ago, and her son had walked it the previous year. This was her year to walk to Santiago. When she mentioned the Pilgrim Mass was beginning, I invited myself along, although neither of us was Catholic.

When it was time for the Eucharist, the priest invited all to participate. In Spanish, he explained that non-Catholics could hold their arms folded across their chest and receive a blessing. I said a prayer of gratitude for my own progress and well-being, and for the strangers and new friends around me.

If I have a tip to share with you from today's walk, it is, "Invite yourself along."

Love,

Dad

DAY TWO:

"Give help when you can, and ask for help when you need it"
Zubiri, September 21

Dear Chase, Noah, and Cara,

As sleepless nights go, last night in Roncesvalles wasn't too bad. Between my jet lag and the snoring from the hundred or so other pilgrims in the albergue, I didn't sleep nearly as much as I would have thought, especially after walking seven and a half hours yesterday. So as the first early risers began to stir to get a start this morning, so did I. Dressing, gathering the few things I had left out of my pack, and filling my CamelBak for the day took only a few minutes, and I was out the door of the albergue with a few other early walkers.

In contrast with the baptism of hiking in the mist up and over the Pyrenees, this morning's hike out of Roncesvalles was dry, flat, and dark. I crossed the street to the footpath where the sign reading *Santiago de Compostela 790 kilometers* sits at the edge of the road. I shined my headlamp on the sign and then down the paved path along the edge of the highway to Burguete. After a few kilometers' walk, I came to the town where Hemingway and his characters spent time trout fishing. There was an open café offering breakfast, and I asked for espresso, which I was corrected to call *café solo pequeño* by the shopkeeper. I ordered a lunch for the road, a *bocadillo tortilla*. A bocadillo is a sandwich made from lengthwise-cut loaves, not sliced bread. A tortilla is an omelet. I chat for a moment with pilgrims at a couple of tables, and then I swing my backpack into place.

At the street corner by the local bank in town, the Way turns right, goes across the Urrobi River, and then runs along pastures where cows graze. I thought for a moment about getting cash from the ATM and decided to do it later tonight.

My backpack still felt solid and good when I snugged up the waist belt. When I was reading about how to pack, some pretrip advice suggested the pack weight should be ten percent of one's body weight. When I weighed it on the airline scale, it was nineteen pounds. With water and a bit of food, it was close to twenty-one. That included your sleeping bag, Noah. Mine was a bit too warm for this time of year.

And Cara, thank you for sewing the flag patches from my other trips on my pack. It's a great conversation starter. Several pilgrims have commented on their home flag or asked about one they don't recognize. After this trip, I'll need to add two more flags. This is the first international trip my backpack hasn't held a camera. After filming documentaries and looking at those seventeen countries from behind a viewfinder, it's nice to have left the camera behind. My pack is like my old cargo pants I wore yesterday; it's lasted through my travels since you and Noah were born.

The ironic pleasure, especially compared to yesterday's misty fog, is that today's hike looked like a travel photographer's dream: small groups of hikers on a trail that winds along pastoral plains and then rises a bit before descending through a woodland into the little town of Zubiri. There were opportunities for breathtaking photos all around, but by my choice, I instead stopped and made a point to turn around and appreciate the full 360-degree view. I suppose I looked like an oddly cast stand-in for Julie Andrews in *The Sound of Music*, singing about the hills being alive.

What's it like walking? At times, there are as many as fifteen to twenty people walking in a line about the length of a city block. That's a guess. I never counted them one by one. A few walk two abreast; most walk single file. Especially when the trail narrows, it's just easier to move one at a time. At other times, there are no other hikers as far as I can see in front or behind me.

The interesting thing about this trail is that it is not just the Camino; it is also a leg of the *Gran Recorrido*, or GR, network of hiking trails. It is used by locals for recreational walks and some mountain bike rides. And not everyone walks. Bicyclists, too, can complete the Camino. And since most people were heading west toward Santiago, it was common for bicyclists to pass me from behind.

But in the middle of the day, I began meeting mountain bikers riding toward me, in groups of two or more. Many of them had a paper map in a holder either on their handlebars, on their arms, or hung from their necks. My best guess was they were in a sporting event.

After about fifty bicyclists zipped by me with stoic determination, one group stopped and asked min English, "Have you seen some people…on bikes…dressed like us?"

"*Si*," I replied. "*Mucho*."

"Which way did they go?"

I pointed. They nodded and peddled away. I smiled in a self-congratulatory way. What do you know? I knew something. I could help. I felt like a local, no longer like the title character of Heinlein's *Stranger in a Strange Land*. I remembered something from college, that the title of Heinlein's book is a reference to Gershom in Exodus 2:22. I made a note in the journal you gave me, Chase, to look it up when I get home.

My tip for the hike today is this: give help when you can, and ask for help when you need it. I gave some (minor) help to the bicyclists, but I was soon reminded that help is both given and taken. By coincidence, Zubiri, my planned stop for the day, was the bicycle rally's start and end point, and it is also where I decided to get more cash.

The ATM was in a local bank branch next door to the albergue I chose for the night. I pressed the buttons on the machine to request two hundred euros and watched as the messages flashed across the screen. I heard the typical clicks as the motor turned the cash-dispensing rollers. The access door opened, then closed. The sounds repeated, and the access door opened and closed again. It did it one more time as if to say, *Okay, last try*. And then everything stopped. The screen displayed a message in English that I read and reread to be sure I understood. Yes, my account had been debited. No, the machine could not dispense cash and to contact my branch.

Every Step is a Gift

I peered in the bank's window. It was closed. This was Saturday, and they would also be closed all day Sunday. By Monday when they opened, I would be another day down the Camino, looking for a pay phone or a computer to contact the bank.

Dejected, I returned to the albergue, a private, well-kept house with a dorm room that included a small balcony overlooking the main street. This albergue is quite a bit different from the IKEA-like space in Roncesvalles. It is a spacious city home with three floors. In the dorm, filled with bunk beds tucked side by side, I met Dan and Maria. He is originally Canadian and is now living in Costa Rica. They are hiking the Camino carrying day packs and sending their larger backpacks ahead using a shuttle company from albergue to albergue. Maria speaks Spanish and English, so I asked for her help. Would she translate a phone call to the bank?

She was willing, but her cell phone did not have minutes for use in Spain, so we set out to borrow a local phone, found a pay phone in a neighboring albergue, and with a combination of dumb luck and euro coins, connected with a helpful person at the bank phone center who reviewed the records. She said that she could see the transaction and that the machine had not dispensed any cash. But to fix the issue, I needed to call my bank in the United States.

So, for now, I'm down two hundred euros, but I think I can work it out Monday when I find a phone and can call the United States. I thanked Maria, and she returned to the albergue to meet Dan. I wandered through the streets of the tiny stop on the Camino.

At the café across the street, I met a French woman, Isabelle. Isabelle and I had what I would call an "international conversation," a combination of French, Spanish, English, and hand gestures. She and the café owner looked at me, smiled, and gave each other knowing looks. They had a rapid exchange in French that ended in laughter. If I were writing one of my novels, I would say they talked about "how good-looking the American is." In reality, I'm sure they said something about "how bad the American smells after hiking all day." Bruised ego aside, I jotted the note in my journal.

The afternoon felt like we were all at home sitting on our front steps, not thousands of miles away on a pilgrimage. Sitting on the curb, Dan and Maria shared a bag of olives with me. Sandra from dinner the night before is staying at the albergue up the street and stopped to talk before going there to make dinner with new friends. Kevin, also from last night's dinner, is camping in a tent next to the river. He and I talked at length while we stood on the bridge over the river.

At dinner in our albergue, Dan and Maria ended up at another table, and I sat with Isabelle and Maxim. Maxim has a thumb-width goatee, is Czech, and works in the Canadian embassy. In English, he said he works in personnel and in IT.

Isabelle spoke a handful of English words, more than my handful of French. Maxim spoke English, French, and Spanish and eagerly served as translator for the table. We drank wine and shared food, and Maxim patiently repeated every question and every answer.

Isabelle began her pilgrimage in Le Puy, France, last year and was completing the second half this year. She hoped to be done in thirty-three days or so. Maxim was pressed for time, so he wanted to be done in twenty to twenty-five days.

"After we get to Santiago, are you going on to Fisterra?" I asked.

Fisterra is on the western edge of Spain and for a while was believed to be the end of the world. In guidebooks and in conversation, it is also called Finisterre. *Yes* for Isabelle; *no* for Maxim.

Isabelle said she planned to burn her clothes there and run into the ocean. Maxim was shocked.

"Yes," I nodded. I had heard of the tradition.

I marvel at the helpful nature of those around me. If the Camino is a metaphor for life, there is no way to know when you will be giving help or needing help. The gift of the Camino is the number of people willing to help and expecting nothing in return.

Love,

Dad

> *Give help when you can, and ask for help when you need it*

Every Step is a Gift

DAY THREE:

"Be open to change"

Zabaldika, September 22

Dear Chase, Noah, and Cara,

The physical logistics of the Camino are really quite simple. You talk, eat, and sleep, all the while walking west to Santiago.

But being a bit more specific, each pilgrim carries a credential. It is a simple accordion-folded card that has blank spaces where a rubber stamp can be marked each time I stop. The credential verifies to albergues and churches that I am, indeed, a pilgrim. As such, I am granted access to accommodations and sometimes discounts.

The credential also proves to the cathedral in Santiago that I walked the required distance. At the pilgrimage's conclusion, if you have walked and if you desire, the cathedral will give you a certificate, called a *compostela*, certifying that you made the journey.

The approximately eight-hundred-kilometer/five-hundred-mile journey can be done in any number of sections or stages. The primary English language guidebook divides the Camino into thirty-three stages. The French Pilgrim Association divides it into thirty-four. Some take more time; others, like Maxim, do it more quickly. Some pilgrims carry everything they need on their backpack. Other pilgrims, such as Dan and Maria, send their bags ahead each day using a transportation company.

The French association lists over a hundred albergues, guest houses, and hotels along the Way. The possible combination of stops and layovers is staggering. What I do, and I think what most pilgrims do, is show up at the day's end and ask about a bed. While it is not necessary or even suggested to have reservations, in this era of cell phones and ubiquitous Wi-Fi, some pilgrims phone ahead from stay to stay. I don't miss having a cell phone or Wi-Fi, but it would be a helpful tool.

The rest of the journey is complicated only by you yourself. If the Camino is a metaphor for life, then, as with life, there is a path you try to follow. On the Camino, that path is marked with traditional signs, an iconic scallop shell, and the ubiquitous yellow arrow. The arrows are most often spray-painted on the road, the side of a building, a tree, a fence post, or a rock. It's a marvel that delinquents and hoodlums haven't painted arrows in false directions. Pilgrims from a number of countries have often shared, "Oh, this would never work in my country." But it works in Spain. And it seems to keep me and my one hundred thousand closest friends on the same path.

Let me put the numbers in perspective. According to the Pilgrim's office in Santiago, around two hundred thousand pilgrims completed the Camino last year. Keep in mind, not everyone walks the Camino in one continuous trip. Some people walk parts each year for several years, so the statistics are a fluid count, tallying only the people who complete the pilgrimage in any given month.

My best guess is that one hundred people started the same day as I did. But even with a hundred of us walking the same way on the same day, spread out over a typical day's walk of twenty-five kilometers (fifteen miles); that averages four people per kilometer. It's not difficult to see how each of us spent much of the day walking alone, occasionally being passed by a faster walker or overtaking a slower one.

On a stretch of road in Zabaldika, I was walking in a stretch by myself, and as I neared a corner, I noticed two women having an animated conversation in Spanish. From their body language and their words, I guessed they were making a joint decision. Upon reaching agreement, one turned and walked to my right and out of sight, and the other woman approached me.

As she came closer, she spoke to me in nonaccented English and in a clear voice as if she were talking only to me. Because we were walking on a narrow street between two buildings, it amplified the sound effect. A movie special effects team couldn't have created the same feeling as I heard her words.

This was not an out-of-body experience. No mystical imagination, no sense of a strange voice in my head. Just a reminder of how clear things can be heard when I reduce the noise in my life.

"You must not follow the arrows," she said to me. "You must turn right and visit the church. It's up a steep hill, but you will have to walk up hill anyway."

I nodded as she continued. "They moved the signs, the Camino used to go right past the church. I'm going now to see why they moved them and to get them to put them back."

You must turn right and visit the church

"Thank you," I said. I think. Maybe I just nodded.

At the corner, I ignored the yellow arrow pointing to the left and followed the woman's advice.

Ugh, uphill—no kidding. Two or three other pilgrims were climbing ahead of me. I joke with myself, saying that instead of meaning *way* the real meaning of *camino* is *up*. Our reward was seeing the church.

At the top of the hill, surrounded by shade trees and a small and tidy lawn, is the Iglesia de San Esteban. Saint Stephen is the patron saint, and the church dates from the thirteenth century. It is home to an order of the Religious of the Sacred Heart of Jesus (RSCJ).

Kind of a surprise to have the same name as the Sacred Heart Church in West Des Moines, where you each joined the faith. And here I was at the invitation of one of the sisters of the Sacred Heart outside the church, ready to walk in. The odd thing is, if I had walked thirty seconds faster or thirty seconds slower, I would have passed the corner, followed the yellow arrow to the left, and missed this church entirely.

Inside the church, I knelt at the pew and then stared for several minutes at the retablo behind the altar. It was a bright and artistic carving of twelve saints and Jesus. The spiritual feeling inside that church was unlike any sense of calm I've felt in my life. And in the calm, I felt an invitation to consider what the church means in my life. This was an invitation from others and from the sister who told me I "must turn right and go to the church."

I paused to pray. I prayed not only gratitude for the help I had received in Zubiri but also for each of the pilgrims I have met along the way: Isabelle, Maxim, Dave, Pam, Kevin, Sandra, Dan, Maria, John, John, Peter, Dave, and Pam. I lit a candle and said a prayer for the three of you at home.

Near the back of the church and near the entry door was a spiral stone stairwell up to the bell tower. I'm not claustrophobic, but the stairs seemed to go on forever as I climbed above the church choir. I didn't know that *choir* is a physical part of the church until I read the note about the building. Finally, I walked onto the wooden plank floor of the bell tower. I read from the sheet of paper given to me by one of the sisters:

Typical of the 13th century, the bell tower rises up from the choir section of the church and is supported by it. Its body is rectangular and the bells are situated in two arched windows. One of the bells, the smallest, bronze one, is said to be the oldest in the whole region of Navarra. It probably belonged to Saint Saviour's Monastery in Asiturri, which was situated, in earlier times, on the other side of the river Arga. It has a beautiful sound.

A sign invited pilgrims to ring the bell, and I did, one time, and it resounded across the valley as I looked out and across to the hills on the opposite side. How many other believers have done this very thing over the last eight hundred years? If all things are connected, I felt I had just connected with them all. This was a shared moment, not about me but about everyone who had done the same thing.

I walked down the spiral stone stairwell and outside, wanting both to end my day and spend the night. I was eager to walk on to see more of what lay ahead.

Before strapping my backpack on in the shade of the lawn, I looked over the papers the sisters gave to me before folding them. The second paper was a half sheet, one side describing the Way as both parable and reality. On the flip side were "The Beatitudes of the Pilgrim." I read them, seeing particular meaning for this stopover in the first one:

Every Step is a Gift

Blessed are you, pilgrim, if you discover the Camino opens your eyes to what is not seen.

Chase, the yellow Rite in the Rain all-weather journal you gave me has become both diary and filing cabinet, so I'm tucking the sheets of paper from the sisters inside the cover.

Love,

Dad

DAY FOUR:

"Walk your own Camino"
　　　　Cizur Menor & Puente La Reina, September 22 and 23

Dear Chase, Noah, and Cara,

Yesterday, after leaving Zubiri, I walked through Pamplona, the first big city on the Camino. The narrow streets were filled with residents, tourists, and pilgrims. The differences in the architecture and layout of Pamplona capture the contrasts and parable of the Camino. Pamplona is a contemporary city of two hundred thousand people. On the eastern side, an arched bridge over the Río Ulzama leads to an arched passage through a building that leads to the modern suburb of Arre, with newer streets and newer buildings reflective of traditional design but with clearly modern materials.

From the other perspective, the very act of walking with all I have on my back is an age-old human experience. Other than clothing, it doesn't look much different in the year 2013 than it did in the year 1013. And once you cross the Bridge Magdalena and pass under the Portal de Franci, the historic city of Pamplona feels like a city of centuries past. The stone walls, the stone streets, and the close quarters of the three-story buildings lining each side are the authentic version of what amusement park designers try to create in their attractions.

It is both past and present. It is historic and modern. It is sacred and secular. Pamplona is important in several contexts of history. Hemingway made it famous in his writing, although the town wryly suggests that it was Pamplona that made Hemingway famous. This is the place known for the annual running of the bulls.

On my way through the city, I walked through the narrow streets and visited the bull ring, the statues of the running of the bulls, and the bust of Hemingway. As the afternoon sun heated the plaza, I stopped and savored some Navarra wine at a small table in the shade of an awning and then continued up the road, along the way meeting several familiar faces and some new ones in the town of Cizur Menor on the western edge of Pamplona at the Albergue Roncal.

We were scattered among patio tables and chairs: the trio of Canadian couples, John, Peter, and John and their wives. Centenie, also from Canada, introduced herself and joined in the chat. She, too, was beginning the Way solo along with one hundred thousand of her closest friends. There was a group from the UK and more than a dozen other pilgrims representing as many countries.

While settling in, I turned into the kitchen area to be greeted by a tall, young, and slender woman from Denmark wearing only her bright red underwear. I quickly turned away, thinking I had come into the wrong room. The pilgrim next to me whispered, "You Americans are too uptight about everything." I guess you can expect to see just about every style of dress or undress.

The conversation tonight included the usual topics: how long and how far each was walking, and where the next stop was in our plans. The UK group was planning to walk for two weeks and then continue the rest of the Way another year.

After dinner, we all returned to bed, and I spent another night listening to the chimes of the church bells. The bells chime once for each hour. They also chime one time at each half hour. So if the church clock chimes three times, it's 3:00 a.m. My insomniac logic kicks in when the clock chimes once. Is it midway through an hour? Or is it 1:00? I begin to wonder, *If you hear it chime once two times in a row, is it 12:30 and 1:00, or is it 1:00 and 1:30?* And just as I begin to drift off, a snore, snort, or gasp from another pilgrim startles me awake. But rather than being grumpy, it causes me to laugh. It's a funny scene from a movie. And it's only a snore; it's not like a cell phone ringing because the caller has forgotten the time zone difference.

This morning, I packed and pulled on my backpack, and I headed in search of a quick breakfast of tostadas and *café solo pequeño*. The restaurant from last night was open early. Outside on the sidewalk, they have large wooden barrels converted into tables and stumps turned into stools, and it gives the modern neighborhood a bit of Old World charm. I think it was early, even by Camino standards. The host behind the bar looked as desirous of coffee as I felt, but his hospitality and generosity were sincere.

With enough café solo to feel awake and still ahead of the dawn, I set out down the red brick sidewalk next to the asphalt road and, with a flick of my headlamp, searched for the arrow pointing to the path leading up the hill to Alto del Perdón. *Alto* means what you think—high—and is used to refer to a high point in the trail or a group of hills. At the top is a collection of wind turbines and the metal statue of the pilgrims where "the wind meets the stars." When the city ended and the country began, I noticed a unique smell—fennel mixed with other organics. And while searching for the arrow, I met Peter and Kath from Australia. We chatted for a while, and as their pace accelerated, we separated, destined to meet again somewhere down the Way.

Just before sunrise, I came upon a solitary stone bench on the side of the trail. It seemed a bit out of place; there was nothing else nearby. My path on the trail was to the south and west, but when I sat down, I faced the ruins of Guendulain in the north and a view of the Pyrenees to the east. As I leaned back on the bench, the sun rose over the mountains. The Sisters of the Sacred Heart beatitudes included this:

Blessed are you, pilgrim, when you don't have words to give thanks for everything that surprises you at every twist and turn of the way.

In a busier time, I would have been focused on the other direction and missed the sunrise. I sat there a while, then moved up the hill, where I asked a fellow pilgrim to take and share my photo to Flickr. In it, I'm wearing my red shirt, and the metal cutout statues are behind me. After the photo, I was off down the trail again with a handful of pilgrims, down a rocky and steep slope, past some vineyards with ripe grapes, and then on to the small village of Uterga, where I caught up with Peter and Kath again at a café.

I took off my backpack and set it on the chair at an open table on the patio in front of the café. There were a few other packs there as well. What is fun is that I'm beginning to recognize backpacks — kind of like recognizing cars in a parking lot. Since we are all on foot and since we are looking in front of us, it becomes easy to identify people from the shape and color of their pack hanging on their back and by any decorations they carry as well.

Maxim, from Zubiri, strolled up as I walked from the inside counter carrying my café solo pequeño and a chocolate croissant. I also had a bocadillo with peppers and ham for later in the day. Maxim's pack was tall and narrow. Peter and Kath each had matching square, full-size backpacks. Peter also wore a smaller day pack on his chest. As he pulled it on, Maxim warned him, "You shouldn't do it like that. Your balance will be off."

Peter, trying not to be offended, replied politely, "Oh really?"

"Yes," Maxim said, looking at Kath's full-size pack before delivering his punchline. "You should wear hers on the front. The balance is better."

Camino humor grows on you.

And Maxim was off again, on his pace to finish in twenty to twenty-five days.

My journal tip for you from today is, *Everyone walks his or her own Camino*. I am beginning to feel what this means. My walk is my walk and my pace, just as it was each of the other's walk and pace. We may begin and end our days with others, but the distance and the trail make it difficult to stay with someone whose pace is different from your own. Some charge up hills and sprint to the next; others take frequent breaks. Some walkers weave side to side; some walk a path that mimics laser precision.

I finished today in Puenta Le Reina. I opted to pass through the old town, cross the historic bridge, and walk the final four hundred meters uphill to the albergue. The albergue is a new modern stone and metal building. I chose it because the guidebook said it had a swimming pool. It does. The *hospitalero*, the man who runs the albergue, said it is closed. I was also the only pilgrim in an albergue designed for one hundred pilgrims.

So I showered, made a pay phone call to the US bank, who quickly returned my wrongly ATM-deducted euros into my account, and opened a bottled water. Today's walk was the shortest of the first four days, about nineteen kilometers (twelve miles). The day ended in a hot, bright sun, and I am happy to be off the road and enjoying the air conditioned comfort of the modern albergue.

The hospitalero asked me about my plans for dinner. The traditional evening meal in Spain is served late, and restaurant service may not start until 8:00 or 9:00 p.m. But to accommodate pilgrims, many restaurants offer a *menu del dia*, or menu of the day. Sometimes called the pilgrim's menu, it is a three- or four-plate meal priced between seven and twelve euros. Some places, such as Roncesvalles, you need to reserve a meal so the chefs can pre-plan. At other stops, you can drop in as early as 5:30 or 6:00 p.m. A typical menu del dia includes a first plate salad, an entree second plate, a third plate side dish, and a fourth plate, dessert. I looked at the menu offered by the hospitalero, made my choices for the night, and thought back to my dinner companions from Roncesvalles. I wondered which of them I will see again.

Where the wind meets the stars, Alto de Perdón

I was smiling over the memory when the second pilgrim for the day walked in to register. It was Sandra from the dinner and Pilgrim Mass. We exchanged greetings and talked about the swimming pool and the fact that it is closed.

By dinner, there were only four of us: Sandra, me, and two sisters from a Boston family. One was an actress, her sister a student. We shared stories of our first four days of walking. Their parents had chosen an albergue in town, and the daughters were staying here. We got on the subject of music and songs, remembering "Me and Bobby McGee" with its memorable line, "Freedom's just another word for nothin' left to lose." We talked about Two Mile, and they asked about farming, about chickens, and about how often a hen laid an egg. I told them nearly every day.

"Every day?!" was the surprised and instantly comical reply.

I think a couple of photos have been posted to Flickr today, including one from a small table at a café bar. I've learned much of our social life on the Camino takes place around the bars because they stay open during siesta when the rest of the businesses in town shut down for a few hours.

Love,

Dad

DAY FIVE:

"Don't judge a city by its siesta"

Estela, September 24

Dear Chase, Noah, and Cara,

In the morning light, there is a preview of a pretty little town named Cirauqui. You see it as you climb the hill after leaving Mañeru, which is just beyond Puente La Reina. Cirauqui will be a hard act to follow for other towns competing for "Quaint Village of the Year." It's a hilltop village with about five hundred residents. The Camino winds through narrow streets and through an arch where pilgrims can add a stamp to their credential. From there, the Way winds down across a Roman bridge and over a Roman road, one of the oldest Roman roads along the way. It's hard to imagine how many people have walked on these same stones in the hundreds of years since they were set.

My ending town for today, Estella, has a beautiful park and some spectacular bridges over the river. I looked at the pilgrims arriving in a loose group and saw that they had what I call the "pilgrim in the headlights" look, a dazed expression of altered reality. I can feel the same look on my own face. Often in the afternoon, my brain works and builds sentences in either Spanish or English, but what comes out of my mouth are slurred grunts and monosyllables. I see others have this problem, too. After drinking water, shedding the backpack, and taking a shower, some sense of human communication returns.

Today's albergue is a parochial one with two rooms and thirty beds on the first floor of a high-rise office building. It must be safe; it's across the street from the civil guard station, a form of the local police.

During my walk around and after my shower, I met the actress and her sister from last night on a small hill overlooking the town. They were waiting for their parents. When their mom arrived, I offered to walk her to the albergue on my way to explore the town.

Estella has a great name and the bridges look great, but as I walked around the narrow streets, all I found were closed and shuttered buildings, for sale signs, *se vende* signs, and very few people. I walked several streets and out of curiosity turned toward busier streets. I heard a siren. I heard and smelled cars and trucks. Ugh. Compared to the rural villages of the first few days, I concluded this was not a pretty place.

> The "pilgrim in the headlights" look, a dazed exprssion of altered reality

So I retreated to the albergue and rested in the courtyard while pilgrims hung their laundry to dry. I listened to stories and watched as a young couple learned some tai chi moves from an older man. The young man looked to be a student of all things alternative. If you were a casting director and you ordered an extra to play the part of the "alternative lifestyle male backpacking across Europe," they would send you this kid in the courtyard. And that is a compliment. He takes his study of tai chi seriously; he was truly in the moment. His girl companion was having a harder day. Her facial expressions showed frustration with nearly everything the kid did and said. She looked tired, but I could tell it was temporary. Tomorrow will be a new day for both of them.

Other people in their twenties from half a dozen countries were eating pasta together under the arbor that serves as both a shelter and clothesline. By face or backpack, I recognized most of the pilgrims. The green backpack with the scallop shell and yellow flower belonged to Sandra. She was chatting with her friend Noél, a young German man, who then joined a group of younger pilgrims. Sandra and I watched and listened to them and commented about how they are the future of the world. Sandra was also typing her blog via cell phone. By imitative instinct, I reached for my phone and remembered I don't have one. I let her type and listened as the young Canadian told a convincing story about the dangers of drop bears…then he moved onto the evils of snow snakes. He's the one who learned of the Camino on Monday, bought his gear Tuesday, and was on a flight Wednesday.

I regret not bringing a device but only for a moment. This is the modern world, and despite the centuries-old churches and walking on stone roads laid by Romans, Spain is as modern as any developed nation. Wi-Fi is everywhere and free. Internet cafés, while they exist, are dwindling because people don't meet or go to borrow a computer; they carry one everywhere.

While a dozen years ago, pilgrims might have worried about getting off the trail early enough to get a bed, the current pilgrims are eager to get an electric outlet to charge their device…or devices. Many have a phone, some a phone and tablet, some a phone and e-book reader. I've seen laptops, full-size camera kits, and long lenses. As I told you in the last letter, everyone walks their own Camino.

The albergue has a tiny and efficient kitchen. It would be a bit cheaper, more fun, and communal to cook a meal to share among friends and strangers. It is equally as fun to go out and dine in the streets of the towns and cities, sample the local fare, and mingle with residents. Even with my less than favorable impression of Estella, Sandra persuaded me to venture out, and what we discovered was that the city comes alive post-siesta. When we walked on the main plaza, the stores were open, and the town of Estella was transformed.

We met the tall Danish woman, who was headed to the pharmacy in search of Compeed to prevent blisters and earplugs to block out the sound of snoring. The group of British pilgrims who are doing the hike in sections were searching for ibuprofen and earplugs. In the square, young children ran free, shouting and laughing. Parents watched casually from the sides and small tables.

Dinner was slow and relaxed, mixed among tables of pilgrims and locals, and there was never a hurry to ask the waiter for the evening's

Every Step is a Gift

bill. It is easy to judge; it is easy to make quick decisions; it is easy to overcharacterize. I do it all the time. But my tip learned after seeing the town of Estella transform is this: don't judge a city by its siesta.

Love,

Dad

DAY SIX:

"Listen for the music"

Los Arcos, September 25

Dear Chase, Noah, and Cara,

Today began and ended with thoughts about music and song. Last week, before I left for the Camino, I sent the final draft of my novel *Kolby Rae* to my editor. It's the story of a country music singer and songwriter in her mid-thirties who is trying to find her way and life in her career. I wrote most of the songs she "wrote." Which is easier than it sounds because many were just hooks — catchy little phrases that I could sprinkle in to give the reader a sense of the song and the character's style. But I still have one song to write. I need a song about falling in love. In the novel, my main character is struggling with her ability to sing this song, and as the author, I'm struggling with my ability to write it. And the creative muse has been silent on the Camino until today.

Walking up a tree-covered path, I stepped to the side and began scribbling some lyrics in my journal:

:: If you kiss me here, I might not know where I'm at ::
:: If you hold me close, I might not ever look back ::

I know, it's not much of a hit song, but it's a start.

Every Step is a Gift

Also in *Kolby Rae*, I am using a famous song by someone else: "Hallelujah," by Leonard Cohen. In the novel, it's a song of personal strength. The singer and her band sing it backstage before every show. So I licensed the lyrics to use in the book. And while walking, I sometimes hum along in time with my steps.

Uphill and a few kilometers out of Estella, the town I stayed in last night, is a wine fountain. It's in a local winery opposite the Monasterio de Irache. The wine fountain is a tapper in the wall of the winery, enclosed in a tiny gated courtyard. To be honest, chilled red wine before sunrise is either too early or too late to drink, I'm not sure which. To keep with tradition, many of us sampled the wine using the scallop shell we carry as a makeshift drinking glass. Fortunately, we all have one. Scallop shells are one of the symbols of a pilgrim on the Camino de Santiago.

Just beyond the fountain, the group of us came to a crossroads of sorts, a choice of paths for the day. The guidebook offers a detour or scenic alternative to the traditional path. The group of pilgrims talked about the differences and then split, some going each way. On other days, I've taken the detour. Today, I wanted coffee more than scenery, so I took the traditional route, with a mix of rural fields and smaller towns. There is a fountain — this time for water — originally built by the Moors and rebuilt within the last twenty years or so. It's a small building covering a pool with two arched entrances and steps down from the trail to the water. I don't think it is safe to drink, but it's humbling to think about the number of people who have stopped here.

Most of today's walk was on a narrow rock and clay trail six to eight feet wide, past some recently cut hay fields. On one of the solitary hills sits the castle of San Esteban near Monjardín. The vineyards seemed a bit smaller than some from a few days ago, but grapes were ripe, and the smell was earthy and sweet, mixed with wild fennel.

Just as today began in song with thoughts about my book and Cohen's "Hallelujah," the day ended in song. A woman was singing in the lobby of the Casa Austria, an albergue just off the Camino in the town of Los Arcos. As I checked in, the hospitalero stamped my pilgrim passport with a red circular stamp with the scallop shell in the center. It's my eighth stamp.

Just down the street from the Casa Austria albergue is the Plaza de

Santa Maria. This plaza is like those in Estella and the previous stops. Tables nearby are filled with friendly faces and familiar smiles. There is a mix of local residents and pilgrims.

So even though the end of the walk today was hot and shadeless along recently mowed hayfields, I wasn't really tired, and I wasn't ready to rest. This is my sixth day of walking. Before I left Iowa, I had a rough plan to walk six days and rest a day. But I've figured out that plan isn't practical. I'm in no rush. My flight home is on November 7. I have plenty of rest days built in to take side trips or explore a city.

My only other plan was to spend thirty-three walking days to reach Santiago, one day walking for each year of Christ's life. Thirty-three years, thirty-three days, thirty-three stages of walking.

So my only two real plans were to walk six days, rest and lay over on the seventh, and to walk a total of thirty-three days to Santiago. It turns out that laying over any day breaks a common albergue rule. Typically, the albergues require you to leave, usually by 8:00 a.m. each morning, and remain out until 1:00 p.m. or later in the afternoon. By custom, they don't allow pilgrims to stay two nights in a row. The other thing I've noticed is that my body really doesn't want to rest. I'm as ready as I was the first day to keep walking. So no rest day tomorrow. Logroño is the next big town on the Way, with a population of 130,000 people.

Love,

Dad

DAY SEVEN:

"Indulge in moderation"

Logroño, September 26

Dear Chase, Noah, and Cara,

The Camino singular is really the Caminos plural. There are several sections of path that lead to Santiago. The most popular in our time is the path I am walking, the Camino Frances. In earlier times, though, other paths have been more popular. And on the Camino Frances, many pilgrims begin as I did in Saint-Jean-Pied-de-Port, France, just across the Pyrenees Mountains.

The Way itself is a string of trails, roadside paths, city streets, and rural roads. As you've read in my earlier letters, the Camino Frances wanders through farmland and vineyards, tiny hamlets, and some of Spain's largest cities: Pamplona, Logroño, Burgos, León, and Santiago. Along the route are public fountains to refill water bottles, small cafés, bars, and restaurants.

Sleeping along the Way can be done by open air camping, as Kevin did, whom I met in Roncesvalles and again in Zubiri. However, the Spanish tradition and culture insists that there be a roof over every pilgrim's head. People have opened their homes to overnight stays by pilgrims, and there are small bed-and-breakfast-style inns, hostels, and hotels. The majority stay an albergues. There are grocery stores, shops of all kinds, and television entertainment, and Wi-Fi is everywhere, along with the modern conveniences of twenty-first-century living.

But walking the Camino, you pass and explore castles, churches, cathedrals, bridges, and roads more than a thousand years old. The contrast of standing in the footsteps of El Cid and Roland while the pilgrim a few feet away uses Google and Wikipedia via a smartphone to read the history is one of the many enjoyable paradoxes lived along the Camino.

This is the morning of day seven, and tonight's pilgrim meal will be in the next large city, Logroño. This morning's walk, like those of the last few days, began in the dark. Spain, oddly, shares a time zone with Germany to the east, so the sunrise is typically later on a clock than other countries on the same longitude. Combining their odd time zone with autumn's naturally later sunrise means that early morning includes walking in darkness using headlamps. A bit like Job in 29:3: *While he kept his lamp shining above my head, and by his light I walked through darkness.*

Standing in the footsteps of El Cid and Roland, using Google and Wikipedia

The weather so far has been ideal. Other than the first day's mist over the mountains, it has been sunny and dry. Just the same, today in Viana, I stopped in a shop and bought a rain poncho. For now, it's tucked away in the bottom of the pack, but I predict I'll use it before long.

Peter, John, and John waved as they turned down the street to the municipal albergue. Later in the Plaza Mercado, I met with Alice from the Netherlands and asked her to take my photo. She insisted I make a duck face. You'll know the photo when you see it. She has an interesting business. She restores and rents gypsy wagons to campers in the Netherlands.

Afternoons and early evenings have become a social hour as we mix and talk with other pilgrims — sometimes new faces, sometimes familiar ones. On the walk into Logroño, a man working in a shared garden space yelled something about a fiesta.

Every Step is a Gift

The town had music stages set up along some of the streets. As the night went on, the crowds moved through the streets, but there was no sign of a fiesta. After dinner at a street-side restaurant, I made my way to bed. Fiesta or no, I was tired. In the journal, I made this note: "Indulge in moderation." It has an ironic double meaning, don't you think?

Love,

Dad

F.R. "Fritz" Nordengren

DAY EIGHT:

"Share your abundance with others"

Ventosa, September 27

Dear Chase, Noah, and Cara,

According to the guidebook, the modern park a few kilometers outside of Logroño had a coffee shop, and sadly, it was not open when I got there. So it was a long haul this morning, about thirteen kilometers (eight miles), before coffee and breakfast. Breakfast was in the town of Navarrete. I sat outside on a balcony seating area that looked down the hill to the rest of the town. The pilgrim at the next table had an iPad and was playing Candy Crush. It's a reminder that everyone walks their own Camino, and I can only imagine how many levels you can win with few distractions and free Wi-Fi. I've seen others with music so loud, you could hear it from the earbuds of their iPods. I met a nudist — she was dressed at the time — who doesn't understand why people are shocked when they meet her on the trail. And there are power hikers, injured hikers, and lots and lots of knee braces.

In Navarrete, before continuing, I stopped at the Iglesia Parroquial de la Asunción de Navarrete. If the retablo from the Church of Saint Stephen was inspiring in its colorful detail, the retablo here is incredibly ornate, made from gold. The style is known as the best example of Rioja Baroque.

The end of today's walk was the town of Ventosa. On the main road, there is a little store with a nice café and outdoor seating. Peter, John, and John were there ahead of their wives. And as pilgrims do, we were all chatting. A new man was with us, originally from Bolivia. He was telling the story of how he came to live in Minnesota.

He was not a handsome man or an ugly one. He had the face of a character actor—round cheeks, a balding head, wide smile, and dancing eyes. If he were on television, he would have a huge following. His storytelling style was self-effacing and likable. He soon had the attention of most of the outdoor diners.

"Why did you move to Duluth?"

"Look at my face," he said with an impish grin. "I am damned."

He told us this was his second Camino. He talked about moving from Bolivia to Minnesota after seeing photos of the Saint Croix River in *National Geographic.*

"I told my wife, 'That is where we should live our life.'"

As a comic comment, someone asked playfully, "And that's when your wife divorced you?"

"No," he said. They are still together. But he shared the phrase he used to describe someone who shared the Camino experience with him on his first trip and how his companion on the Camino had his heart. His wife had his heart at home, and on the Camino, his companion had his heart. If the Sacred Heart of Jesus represents Jesus's divine love of humanity, perhaps the shared Camino heart represents the pure love the people who are bound together on the Camino also share. His words struck not only me but I think many of the others as well.

Ventosa is a pretty town on a hill, and the albergue is a beautifully restored home, with music playing, elaborate tile, incense, and comfortable bunk beds. There is a large courtyard and a big kitchen. The young couple who were learning tai chi in Estella is here. Alice from Logroño is here, along with Bitte and Sandra.

The women decided to make dinner for the four of us. We each struggled with the flat surface cooktop, pushing, pressing, and swiping our fingers over the controls to get them to work. Nearly everyone in the kitchen tried their hand—sorry for the pun—at turning on the burners. Finally we figured out the right swipe and touch to make the

F.R. "Fritz" Nordengren

burners heat.

The young couple looked tired and hungry. They had some small portions of food, and I couldn't help but notice their eyes as they looked at the large meals others were making. They finished their meal, and we carried our food to an outside table.

I didn't think about it until after we finished our own meal and I looked at what remained in the pan. We should have invited them to our table. I asked my tablemates if they minded if I shared with the couple, and they all quickly agreed.

The look of joy and gratitude on their faces was a free and honest expression of emotion. I don't know their story, but I'm guessing they had a set and meager budget for each day. If shelter cost more, the food budget was smaller. I reflected on my own abundance—the things I have, the ATM cards, the friends around me willing to share their food. Before going to bed, I made this note about the day, and I want to pass it on to you:

Share your abundance with others.

Love,

Dad

DAY NINE:

"Dine with the locals"

Cirueña, September 28

Dear Chase, Noah, and Cara,

My most social night to date took place in probably the least likely town. In contrast to the pretty towns of Ventosa and Cirauqui, the pilgrims who walked through this town, named Cirueña, described it as a ghost town. I kept an open mind, thinking back on Estella and day five. Maybe we were just there at the wrong time of day. Or year. It was windy, it was beginning to look like rain, and the first sign of life was a golf course and clubhouse. The buildings looked new. The course looked well maintained, and it was surrounded by rows of neat, nondescript townhouses that looked vacant. Perhaps it is a summer resort town where by the end of September the residents had returned to their lives.

This was Saturday night, in Cirueña.

The overnight options were between the albergue and a private home, a *casa rural*. The casa rural had small bedrooms, and I ended up in a pretty room upstairs with four beds. By midafternoon, all four beds were claimed—one by me, one by Sandra, and two by new friends Lisa and Bernard. Lisa is Australian, and Bernard is French. Lisa and Bernard had been walking together for a few days, and as they unpacked, Lisa exclaimed she had a blister.

She took a deep breath—and joked she hyperventilated—as Bernard willingly lanced the blister. There is an unspoken rule that we don't take comedic pleasure from a fellow pilgrim's hardship, but all of us agreed it was a bit funny. Hungry and tired, the four of us wandered across the street to the café bar. The café had the look and feel of a local neighborhood café. It lacked some of the pilgrim decoration and multilanguage signs. There were residents around us, not pilgrims, and they welcomed us.

Bernard was funny, though he spoke mostly French with a smattering of English. He told stories in pantomime that kept us laughing.

Lisa recounted her daily progress: she and Bernard made a habit of thirty-kilometer days. The four of us would make great travel companions, but they are on a faster pace, and I recall my lesson from day four in Puente La Reina: everyone walks his or her own Camino.

One beer became two. Then we decided to eat. Being voted the best Spanish speaker at the table—an award not unlike calling Dopey the tallest of the seven dwarfs—I asked the man behind the bar about ordering.

"*A las siete.*"

"*Siete?*"

"*El cocinero estará aquí a las siete.*"

I returned to the table. "He says the kitchen opens at seven when the cook gets here."

The pilgrims with watches or cell phones looked and groaned.

"That's two more hours."

We ordered more beer and red wine, in Spanish *vino tinto*.

Bernard got funnier.

Sandra reminded everyone that in Logroño, she asked the other pilgrims sitting at her table what the English word *tipsy* means.

Lisa tried to explain it along a continuum. "Tipsy is"—she wrapped her arm around me and in a mock drunk slur said, "I love you guys." She dropped her arm and leaned back in her chair. "Pissed is passed out on the floor."

Bernard pantomimed drinking from a bottle and then crossed his eyes. We concluded everyone at the table was tipsy.

The café was filling up. The owner of our casa rural was there. He was chatting with two other men. The other tables were full with locals as well; perhaps they owned some of the empty-looking townhomes. Another couple of pilgrims were at the next table,

At 7:00, the man behind the bar picked up his pad and walked toward our table when he was shortstopped by the other pilgrims, who began desperately trying to order from the menu in English. They couldn't decide. The man with the pad looked over to us. I read his expression as apologetic that he was not taking our order.

But he did come, we did order, and we had a wonderful dinner in a local pub far from the pilgrim trail.

After dinner, and maybe after more wine — I don't remember — we walked across the small plaza and into the casa rural and to our shared four-bed bedroom.

Bernard had one more story. He pantomimed drinking and then raised one leg and hopped across the floor, trying to remove his hiking boot.

"Wow," I told them, "the DUI test in France looks really tough."

I thought about the meals we've shared and the people who make their life serving food and refreshment to pilgrims. Sure, it's a job, an income, a business with a hundred thousand customers walking by each year. But I have a respect and appreciation for their service. A town like this is in the middle of the page of the guidebook, meaning it's a rest stop, not an overnight for many pilgrims who are intent on doing it by the book. The German guidebook doesn't break the trek into stages, and the handouts from the French Pilgrim Office likewise have the town between stage end points. It's in between stage nine on the French handout and stage eight on the English book.

Lisa and Bernard have been great company, and the night's meal has planted an idea in me to stop short of or just beyond the stops in the guidebook to seek out surprises and treasures. The handout from the French side lists 195 albergues, and I'm staying in only thirty-three between Saint Jean and Santiago. This stay, midway between stages and in a café for town residents, was a great reminder that I'll share with you as you travel in your life: dine with the locals.

Love,

Dad

DAY TEN:

"The shortest distance between two cafés is a straight line"
Belorado, September 29

Dear Chase, Noah, and Cara,

After ten days and 216 kilometers, I've found a natural rhythm to the day and some mind games I've learned to play, both for encouragement and enjoyment. It would be easy to push on daily at a pace set by someone such as Maxim, intent on reaching the goal in a set number of days. And at times, I catch myself doing that. Not that I am as fit as he is nor as young, but I walk at a fast pace.

So to slow down and to enjoy, I try to stop at every café or bar I come to. Well, not every one. In towns or where there are collections of cafés, I choose one, but it's quickly become the Camino de café. We take turns buying drinks and snacks for each other along the way. We all learn who drinks café americano, café solo pequeño, café con leche, or *Kas Limon*, a Spanish soda with lemon juice. If the chocolate croissants are fresh, we'll share one. If not, a bocadillo cut in half, part for now, part for later down the road.

Many mornings, the albergue does not offer a breakfast, so the primary purpose of the guidebook becomes, how far do we walk before coffee?

But just as often when I come to a town, I am feeling called to also step into the local church. Many of these are smaller buildings than our barn at Two Mile Ranch; others are large cathedrals and famous churches.

One of the gifts of the Camino is that you can approach it from so many perspectives. A church historian could walk the Camino for days, perhaps walking it several times, to see the history and story of the churches. A scholar of architecture could look at the styles and progression of building over the last one to two thousand years. My lack of knowledge and expectation leads me to surprises.

Tonight's dinner and sleep are in Belorado. The albergue is home to a very nice restaurant. In the stairwell hangs a huge poster-size photo of the owners wearing chef's attire. They seated us at small tables for four or six people, and I met Karen from Australia, who is walking with Jennifer from New York. They met earlier on the trail and are walking together. We agreed the food was some of the best of the pilgrim's meals we have had so far on the walk.

"I'm going to walk the world," was what he told me

The walk to Belorado takes us through Santo Domingo de la Calzada and the most famous chicken coop of the Camino. Saint Dominic, the patron saint of Spanish civil engineers, is known for spending his life making the paths, bridges, and roads of the Camino. He was born nearly a thousand years ago, and visiting his town is a reminder of how connected to generations of pilgrims we are as we pass through.

The chicken coop is in the rear of the cathedral because of the story of the miracle of the cock. It's a wonderful fable of a jilted lover, a local girl who meets a young boy on pilgrimage. When their relationship sours, she places a silver goblet in his backpack. He travels on, and she tells the authorities of his "theft." He is arrested and, unknown to his parents, is tried and hanged. His parents return and, finding him still alive, rush to the local sheriff who, in the midst of his midday chicken dinner, proclaims their son is no more alive than the cock on his plate. The chicken stands up and crows loudly, and the sheriff rushes to cut down the boy.

I reflected on that story on the walk into Belorado. There is a common saying among pilgrims: "The Camino always provides." It's hard for me to comprehend miracles on a grand scale, a miracle of Biblical proportion, or the kind of miracle necessary to become a saint. Yet I see examples and hear stories of smaller-world miracles daily on our hikes.

For example, at dinner in Roncesvalles the first night of the Camino, I met Kevin. Kevin sat at the far end of the table. It was nearly impossible to have a conversation with him without shouting and disrupting everyone else, so we spoke the next day on the small stone bridge overlooking the Arga River into Zubiri. Kevin was staying in a tent and was telling me the story of leaving his Chicago home, essentially selling everything and setting out to hike in the Alps. He had an iPad and his tent, and he told the story of being high in the Alps and having to hike down the mountainside to gather food and return to his tent. Perhaps he exaggerated the distances or the exact conditions, but nonetheless, it made for a great story.

Kevin's tent was old. The fabric was torn, and he shared that the poles were broken, mended, and now failing. Yet something had called him to walk the Camino. From his iPad, he searched for a replacement tent. He picked out a brand-name tent, slightly larger than the one he had. When he saw the price, he realized that buying it meant he would be committed to walking.

"I'm going to walk the world" was what he told me, meaning he would walk for the duration of his retirement. He had been in the music business and publishing business, and I got the sense he had worked in the investment business. Now he was walking. His comment reminded me of the character Jules in Quentin Tarantino's *Pulp Fiction*. Jules tells his gangster partner of his retirement and his intent to "walk the world."

Kevin is the first real-life version of "walk the world" I have met so far on this trip. He continued the story about beginning the Camino and arriving in the albergue in Roncesvalles. In addition to being a welcome rest at the end of the day, for many pilgrims, getting to the albergue was a chance to dump unneeded or heavy gear from their kits. There was a table filled with items—hiking poles, clothing, books, cookware—marked with a hand-printed sign: FREE.

It was there that Kevin found a tent. "The exact make and model I had been looking at online," he told me. Then he continued, "I asked the man, 'What's the story with this tent?' And the man replied, 'It's free. Do you want it?'"

That was Kevin's story. So he took the gift from another pilgrim via the free table in Roncesvalles and took it as a sign to walk the world.

"The Camino provides," he said.

Others would tell me Kevin's story, too, adding, "Saint James provides," or "Saint Dominic provides."

Or God.

Miracles. Of all sizes.

Love,

Dad

DAY ELEVEN:

"Every step is a gift"

Ages, September 30

Dear Chase, Noah, and Cara,

I've noticed that while most of the pilgrims are with someone or a group of people at the end of each day, few of us walk "with" someone on the trail. People traveling together walk within sight of each other, but other than the honeymoon couple from Israel and a group of Italians who seem to walk four abreast continuing their never-ending conversation, couples, families, and friends tend to spread out during the day. The family from Boston arrived at albergues at different times, telling the story that one time the mom, with her earbuds in place, became so engrossed in her music, she walked past their agreed-upon stop. The rest of the family took a taxi in search of her.

The family I met today on the Camino is from California: David, Sylvia, Beth, and Sarah. David noticed the Iowa patch on my pack, and we struck up a conversation. I think we were crossing a stream or small river and headed up the hill on the other side,

Walking is a bit like dancing—some people make great partners and others, well, not so much. On the walk from Belorado, I walked much of the way with David. I don't remember everything we talked about, but it was a great section of walking and talking. His father had come from Iowa and then settled in California. We talked about Iowa's famous Maid-Rite sandwich and about our work and jobs.

David has a casual smile and a confident stride. He looks like he belongs on the trail, as I guess many of the others do who have walked these past ten days.

I thought back to one of the papers given to me by the sister of the Sacred Heart in Zabaldika—"The Way: Parable and Reality." Midway through, it read, "The Camino makes you brother/sister. Whatever you have you must be ready to share because even if you started on your own, you will meet companions."

David's a great companion, as are the rest of his family. Everyone I have met along the Way has been great to spend time with and share with. David is moving ahead to catch up with his family, and I had lunch in my pack.

While we were hiking along the beech-tree-lined path, I told David I was going to stop for a lunch break and I would see him down the road.

After a few minutes, I saw a familiar green backpack and recognized Sandra, who was taking a slow pace today because of knee pain. She told me at one of the stops she was having a bad day, saying, "Today the backpack and I are not friends." The trail had finished a gradual climb, and then we were facing a series of three climbs up and down, one hundred meters each.

I waved Sandra over and offered to share my lunch. I don't know if it cheered her up. I've had my share of bad days in life; you probably know this. And somewhere along this stretch of trail, along this metaphor for life, I began to understand something. No matter what the surroundings, the circumstances, the weather, the mood, some days are just bad days.

It struck me as we talked over lunch that, in my life, in all our lives, every step is a gift. In a journey of a million steps, it's easy to overlook a step here or a step there, but every step counts, and every step is a gift.

This is day eleven, and I have twenty-nine days left to walk.

We walked on to Ages, ending the day in a small albergue, catching up with David, Sylvia, Beth, and Sarah. The albergue smelled of something wonderful that has been cooking most of the day. We were treated to an amazing paella.

The hospitalero, in a form of what Cara calls "dad humor," came to our table at the end of the meal and asked if anyone would like "a little more." "*Un poquito?*" he asked, looking at me.

"*Sí*," I replied, thinking that a bit more would be the perfect end to a really good meal.

I got the feeling this was not his first rodeo; he returned with the funny grin of a practical joker, holding a tiny saucer and a teaspoon full of paella. We could tell this was his favorite joke to play on pilgrims.

Every step is a gift.

Love,

Dad

DAY TWELVE:

"When in doubt, push on"

Burgos, October 1

Dear Chase, Noah, and Cara,

Burgos, a city of 175,000 people, is smaller than Pamplona. I hadn't given Burgos much thought. I had not studied the history of the city or the cathedral to know how significant it was. What I didn't figure out by reading the guidebook, not that it mattered, was that the choice of three paths into Burgos each includes a lengthy hike along city streets and a need to be traffic aware. After walking in the rural countryside, getting used to looking both ways before crossing the street took a little practice.

The walk was also complicated by rain—not just mist but the first real rain of the walk. The decision point for which path to take came at a chain-link and barbed-wire fence at the edge of the grass surrounding the Burgos airport runway. A pilgrim was standing there, trying to make sense of the conflicting arrows and choose his path into the city. A few pilgrims were behind me, and we all looked at our guidebooks to pick one of the paths. One or the other might be slightly longer or shorter, but three hundred meters didn't really make a huge difference today. The rain began to fall harder.

The group of us, maybe six pilgrims, failed to reach any consensus and went separate ways. The rest of the walk into Burgos was rainy, wet, and a long slog.

It was only a twenty-two-kilometer day, an easy thing to write on day twelve, with 264 kilometers (164 miles) completed. I shared the walk with Sandra, and a few minutes later, we caught up to Centenie, whom I met on day four in the albergue outside of Pamplona. She was walking on the opposite side of the busy urban thoroughfare, but she was just as rain soaked and just as eager to end the day's walk as we were. To be honest, I thought about giving up for the day and stopping somewhere to sit out the rain, but the sight and stoic determination of both Centenie and Sandra kept me walking. And by afternoon, I was dry and a bit rested, and the rain had stopped.

David told me he had planned dinner after everyone would have had a chance to walk through the cathedral. He said there was free admission for pilgrims with their credential, so after spending so much time in the local churches, I decided to see the cathedral, too.

When I walked inside, I was surrounded by pilgrims and tourists from nations all over the world. We were all silent — not just silent in the sense of "you are in a church" silent, but for the first time in my life, I truly appreciated the word *awestruck*.

The tall ceilings, the artful stained glass, the centuries-old craftsmanship. No one was speaking. The cathedral chapels were filled with a reverent hush, with only the occasional shuffle of feet across the large stone tiles.

I caught up to Sandra just as she stepped on one of the stones. It was loose and not level, so as she stepped, the sound of the loose tile shifting echoed in the Chapel of Saint John of Sahagún. Sandra turned to me and in her best English said, "Indiana Jones."

Her comment brought smiles and nods from everyone nearby who was seeking a way to express their reactions to being immersed in the centuries-old chapel's beauty.

Outside the cathedral, David's daughter Beth offered me a snack of Corn Nuts. The crunchy, salty taste made for a great afternoon treat. So now I have three snack foods to hunt down in grocery stores: olives like I shared with Dan and Maria; Choco Prince cookies, which Sandra calls Prince Rollie; and Corn Nuts, thanks to Beth.

While we gathered outside the cathedral entrance, we became a party of eight. Down the street at the restaurant picked by David, some local men were playing cards at the front table but quickly gave it up, and the waitress moved us in. Sylvia translated, the waitress spoke some English, and we ordered.

The waitress told us *cordero* is beef, and then the entire table acted out a pantomime of farm animals as we sorted through entrees of beef, pork, and lamb. I'm certain from my high school Spanish that cordero is lamb, but I kept that to myself. We looked as if we were acting out the book I read to you kids time and time again: "The sheep goes *baa*; the cow goes *moo*; three singing pigs go *la-la-la*."

We're an international group: David; his wife; Sylvia; his two daughters, Beth and Sarah; Sandra; Brett from New Zealand; Centenie; and Ralph from Germany. The conversation and the laughter began when we sat down and lasted until we all left for the night. Ralph is ending his Camino for this year, and Brett is taking a detour to Madrid. The others are continuing on to Santiago. Some are still unsure if they will go beyond to Fisterra and Muxía.

Slogging through the rain, the wind, and the city traffic today and then enjoying the amazing cathedral and wonderful dinner made my daily advice to you easy to understand. When in doubt, push on.

Love,

Dad

DAY THIRTEEN:

"The things you carry on your back are your fears"
Hornillos, October 2

Dear Chase, Noah, and Cara,

The walk out of Burgos with better weather seemed as long as the hike into Burgos, and there were four of us: Helen, Frank, Sandra, and I. Sandra met Helen earlier in the trail. She is from the UK. Frank is from Oregon. Both Helen and Frank looked familiar, but I don't recall where our paths crossed earlier in the trip. Frank shared homemade beef jerky, both out of kindness and a desire to lighten his pack. He told us the weight of his back; it was nearly double the weight of mine, and he was eager to shed weight by getting rid of the extras.

Frank reminds me of my friend Jim, who, along with Tim, had lunch with me before I left for the Camino. At lunch, Jim told the story of hiking the Appalachian Trail in Maine and meeting a friend the night before he left, having the friend go through his pack and toss aside things such as deodorant and other unneeded luxuries to lighten it.

Frank and Jim both have the same positive attitude. We talked of many things—the Camino stories, the stories of the big and little towns along the way. Frank shared a quotation he's heard: "The reason your pack is so big—everything you carry in there are your fears."

I like the simplicity and logic as I reflect on the things in my own pack and the things I've seen in others'. I've seen mobile phones, iPads, iPods, cameras, hair dryers, every imaginable type of clothing, tents, sleeping pads, sleeping bags, ponchos, gaiters, hiking poles, and first aid kits.

I think about my own kit. I had two hats; I've lost one in the wind. I have both Noah's sleeping bag and a liner — and the liner would have been more than enough. I left a sleeping pad at home in my last-minute weight shedding. However, Noah, your sleeping bag is too big, and if I can find a smaller one, I'll swap out for it. I'll get you a new one when I get back.

It would be possible to do the Camino with much less. But we each have our fears to carry. It plays out in real life, too. The baggage we carry with us, physical or emotional, represents our fears, what we keep close to keep safe. Fear of not looking our best or feeling our best or being unprepared.

The walk today enters the Meseta, the high plains that make up north central Spain. There are a few towns and a few scenic views. At a wayside fountain and park, the pilgrims having lunch were greeted by both rain and flies — herds of flies hovering and following each hiker up the hill and then down the descent into Hornillos.

Hornillos is a tiny town with a nice church and a municipal albergue. And flies. I overheard Peter tell Kath that it reminded him of home, and then he joked, "What flies?"

Jennifer and Karen checked into the albergue before siesta and at mid-siesta, there was no hospitalero to take money, so Jennifer suggested that those waiting take a bed now and sort it out later. The albergue filled, and those waiting were fortunate when the hospitalero opened an annex in another building and had a bed.

The group of pilgrims has shuffled again. There are still familiar faces, but I'm reunited with people I haven't seen in a few days. A woman named Monique — I don't think I've ever met someone with that name — was talking with a group of young hikers including Noél and the Canadian who made the rapid decision to hike the Camino and warned others of "drop bears." Jennifer and Karen are here, as is an older pilgrim whom others call Buen Camino. He is American but has this trail name because he greets everyone with an authentic and original-sounding "Buen Camino." As trail names go, it's about as positive as you can have.

After tonight's dinner was an amazing lightning show. It was far off in the distance at a high altitude, and we all sat and watched the continuous pattern of cloud-to-cloud lightning dance across the sky. A few pilgrims called it heat lightning. We were too far to hear thunder, but at times we could hear something that sounded like distant radio static. I watched it for twenty minutes before heading to bed, and it showed no sign of getting closer or letting up. I think there is a name for this kind of storm. Sailors have reported it on the ocean. It's a stunning display. I didn't even think of photographing it. I guess I am finally comfortable without my cameras.

Today is October 2nd, and I'm told it is the Feast of the Guardian Angels. If I have a guardian angel on this Camino, it is likely Sandra, but along with her are David, Peter, John, and John. They all seem to come into my walk at the right moment. And even after this many days, when I can go for a day or two without seeing one of them, I will come around a corner of the path or sit down at a table and there is one of them with a smile, a story, a joke, or just a quiet nod.

I remembered one of the beatitudes from the paper given to me by the Sisters of the Sacred Heart.

Blessed are you, pilgrim, when you contemplate the Camino and discover it is full of names and dawns.

Love,

Dad

DAY FOURTEEN:

"Don't lose yourself along the way"

Castrojeriz, October 3

Dear Chase, Noah, and Cara,

This morning I woke up with a nagging memory. Actually, a nagging lack of memory. This is day fourteen, and while I have your letters and my notes, the last fourteen days are a bit of a blur. Off the top of my head, I couldn't remember the name of the albergue in Ventosa, or was it Cirueña? Burgos had the cathedral, but was the large plaza in Estella or Los Arcos?

Already, some of the names and faces of pilgrims and hospitaleros are blurring into the background. The good news is, today's walk was a simple four-stop and twenty-kilometer hike to Castrojeriz across the Meseta. The first coffee stop in a café was after ten kilometers—two or three hours of walking. I held out hope that there was a chance of caffeine redemption at a small albergue before that in San Bol. The refuge in San Bol is a quiet escape, powered by a diesel generator with room for ten. It would have been an impressive view of last night's lightning storm from there. But there was no restaurant or café, so the first coffee was in Hontanas.

The Hontanas stop was beautiful. As a broad contrast, in the earlier hilly portions of the Camino, towns were at the tops of hills, probably to make them defendable in the Middle Ages and earlier. From the high point, you could see invaders from far off. In the Meseta—the broad, flat land—the opposite is true. The towns seem to be in the valleys. I am only guessing, but I wonder if it is because the rain and groundwater flows to the lower points. Hontanas is on the down side as the road slopes down a gentle hill.

The albergue is on the right, and the church is on the opposite side of the road. Jennifer and Karen were already there. As I sat down at a table, I looked over to see Karen having an animated conversation with her backpack, which was in the chair next to her. I watched her for a moment and realized she was not talking to her backpack, but rather her backpack was propping her mobile phone and she was having a video chat with her family in Australia. Sandra was there, talking with some pilgrims in German, and two men are talking with a woman. They spoke in English for several minutes before one of the men said he was from the Netherlands. He had heard of a woman from the Netherlands and was hoping to meet her.

The woman replied that she was from the Netherlands, and then they laughed and asked why they were speaking in English instead of Dutch. She moved on down the road after saying goodbye, and the men returned to pilgrim watching.

"Here comes Monique. Look, look, she is wearing pink today."

It was a lighthearted and playful stop.

The church was closed. I would have liked to have started today in prayer. San Bol would have been a nice overnight stop. This albergue would have been nice, and this church would have been a nice place to pray.

I can tell that this Camino experience is going to pass by quickly, with only twenty-six days remaining. There are so many possible things to do and see each day that it would be easy to fill ninety days—the length of a tourist visa—with things to do and see and experience.

In three more stops, we're in Castrojeriz, where Frank found a restaurant whose owner has walked the Camino several times along several paths. Frank has a better taste for wine than the rest of us at the table and asked the waiter to bring a bottle that was *mejor—better* in Spanish. The waiter willingly brought it, and Frank gave us all a broad smile when he tasted it. He shared the wine with us all.

There is also a sporting goods store, where I found a slimmer sleeping bag—about a third of the size of yours, Noah, so I bought it and donated your bag at the municipal albergue. It will keep someone warm who doesn't have one. As we walked around the tiny town, Helen told me about her home, a small cottage about the size of the cabin at Two Mile. We swapped stories about living in small spaces.

As the night and conversation flowed, I also thought about the day and the now scattered mental memory of the past days. Most of my time on other trips has been behind a viewfinder, taking notes, making stories and images. A nightly review of the day's work made it easy to serialize the trip. But I planned this Camino with those tools left behind. I have a journal, but I have found that my hastily scrawled notes in the guidebook are more meaningful than anything else but not quite detailed. These letters are the best chronology of the trip.

If I have a conflict on this pilgrimage, it is that I'm torn between letting the experience flow over me and trying to capture it. Being totally honest, I'm not sure of my place in this story: do I belong in front of the viewfinder or behind the viewfinder? This is one of those times when I don't have much how-to advice other than a broad reminder: don't lose yourself along the way.

Love,

Dad

DAY FIFTEEN:

"Beauty is in the surprises and unplanned"

Frómista, October 4

Dear Chase, Noah, and Cara,

I began today's letter near the top of the hill just outside of Castrojeriz. I was sitting in a modern lean-to shelter on the side of the road on the Alto Mostelares. It was a good place to wait out the rain and watch the sunrise. Down the trail, I could see the bobbing white glow from a pilgrim's headlamp as he made his way to the top.

On the downhill side, the trail changed from crushed stone and dirt to a wide paved path, probably to prevent erosion, but the view was stunning. There was a rapid decline of about one hundred meters in a one kilometer distance. From the high point, you can see beyond the end of the slope and across the flat Meseta for another four or five kilometers. The trail snakes to the trees and along the Pisuerga River in the distance.

The first stop of the day for coffee was in a town on the river: Itero de la Vega. *Itero* is a common place name. It doesn't have much of a translation. The guidebook suggests it is a derivative of the word *hito*, which means landmark or boundary stone. The bridge into the town has eleven arches and is also the border between Castilla and León.

In a coffee shop there, Sandra returned the favor of my lunch gift on day eleven and ordered both coffee and breakfast for me. I think she could sense my need for a rest. To borrow her phrase, today the backpack and I were not friends.

While sitting at the table, I listened to a story told by a woman about eighteen years old. She had missed the ATM in Castrojeriz, had run out of cash, and had spent much of the end of yesterday trying to find either a place to stay for free or an ATM to withdraw money. She ended up hiking to an albergue that was available by donation. She found both a bed and a meal and was on her way to Frómista today, stopping for breakfast. She had been on the phone with her mother.

Her resourcefulness makes me proud of the three of you. I think if you were in a similar situation, you would be smart enough to figure out what to do. And while it makes me nervous to think about it, I know you will be in situations like this in your own life.

I wrote before that I didn't have much of a plan beyond walking for six days and resting on the seventh, which didn't really work out, and walking thirty-three days to reach Santiago. So far, each day I have had a general idea of how far I planned to walk. Today was no different, and I didn't have an albergue chosen for the night's stay in Frómista.

The tree-lined path in the setting afternoon sun along the very still and smooth water in the canal was a surprise. With no plans of where to stay, I looked at some road signs, each listing the name of an albergue and an arrow pointing in the general direction. I smile as I think about explaining my idea of a "plan" to walk the Camino. It plays in my mind like a parent talking to a teenager:

Where are you going?
    On a walk.
How far?
    I'm not sure.
Who are you walking with?
    It depends.
What time will you get there?
    I don't know. I don't have a watch.

The parent in me says today's lesson for the three of you is, "Do as I say, not as I do." But I know you'll do as I did many times in your life.

There are two historic churches here, the Iglesia de San Martin and the Church of San Pedro. The guidebook and the history buffs in the group point out that the town was home to a number of hospitals in the Middle Ages, including one that was a hospital for pilgrims to the Holy Land. Back in the day, Holy Land pilgrims carried a symbolic palm leaf different from the symbolic scallop shell Santiago pilgrims, including me, have carried since Roncesvalles.

There are some who call the pilgrimage to Santiago "The Way of the Sword," where you battle your fears and overcome your demons. The pilgrimage to Rome is called "The Way of the Heart," not of romantic love but of Divine love. The final pilgrimage of the trilogy is that to Jerusalem, "The Way of the Soul." There are a couple of routes to Rome. (What is the saying—all roads lead to Rome?) The distance from Santiago to Rome is 2,600 kilometers, and at the pace I am walking now, it would be a journey of one hundred days or longer, and then from there to the Holy Land by foot or by boat. I've walked fifteen days and covered 330 kilometers (205 miles), and I'm not yet halfway to Santiago.

The man with the trail name Buen Camino is staying at one of the other albergues. He told me he's following in his wife's footsteps. She walked the Camino years earlier. He quickly tells pilgrims that story, how she relays e-mail messages to him. He's in his seventies, fit, and keeping a pace that makes many of the twenty-something pilgrims envious.

My albergue is much more like a guest house than an albergue. The owner wants us all to stay out of the courtyard grass. I didn't understand what she said, but the nearest my Spanish will let me guess is that it is wet from the rain or the ground is too soft. But still, even staying off the lawn, the accommodations are homey.

In my journal, I wrote, "Beauty is in the surprises and the unplanned."

Love,

Dad

DAY SIXTEEN:

"Giving of yourself is sacred"

Carrión de los Condes, October 5

Dear Chase, Noah, and Cara,

I made the decision today to stop and spend a day resting. I'm not physically tired, and I don't have any leg, back, or knee complaints. The few minor blisters I developed have resolved easily, but the last sixteen days of walking are jumbled in my head, so I made the decision to stop and spend an extra day here in Carrión de los Condes.

There is a beautiful park here by the river and an adjacent campground. There are two albergues. My plan is to stay at one, then the other if I'm unable to extend my stay to two nights. We arriving pilgrims are greeted by the sisters of Santa Maria at the door with a tea and small sandwich.

I'm not sure I can put into words what happened next or begin to capture my feelings, but let me share the story with you.

Across the small plaza from the albergue and church, contemporary music played from a bar loudspeaker, and a man was sketching the plaza. As he finished, he asked the pilgrims around him to sign the page with their name and date "so I can remember who was with me."

He asked for my name as well. As I wrote my name, I noticed a man walk past us and into the bar. There was nothing out of the ordinary about him. He was dressed as a pilgrim, and I probably would not have remembered him except that further down the road near the church, I had watched a dog cross the street, chained to a backpack. The dog started walking up the street toward the bar. I don't know why, but I connected the dog and the man. So I got up from the table, and I walked into the bar, looking for the man as my eyes adjusted from the bright day to the darker interior. I found the man holding a plastic bowl and asked him, "*Usted tienes perro?*"

He looked back at me with a pilgrim-in-the headlights look, then looked beyond me as my poor Spanish and his brain figured out what I was saying. Around his neck was a laminated plastic sign that in English read:

I am hiking to Rome and Jerusalem for peace.

Reading the English words, I switched to English. "Do you have a dog?"

I didn't get the sense that either English or Spanish was working. Then his face showed some understanding. He walked out, found the dog, and walked back down the street to the church.

I sat there thinking about his burden. I'd been thinking about the burden each of us carries. If our packs are our fears, our burdens are our responsibility.

Hiking with a dog was this man's burden. A gift, but with responsibility.

I crossed the plaza and saw the dog and backpack safely anchored to a bench and the pilgrim gone, so I continued down the side of the plaza on to my albergue.

As I neared the entryway, I heard Leonard Cohen's "Hallelujah." An odd coincidence. After all, this was the song in my head from *Kolby Rae*, the song I think about as I have walked these past days and miles.

When I stepped inside, the sisters were sitting in a line, with two teenage girls in the middle, one playing guitar, the other holding a cell phone displaying the lyrics. As they sang each verse, they were joined on the chorus by the thirty or more pilgrims, sitting on benches lining the staircase and looking over from the second level.

Having used that song in a dramatic way in my novel and having heard the lyrics, as have so many people around the world, I felt that to be together and sharing that moment was the purest unrehearsed expression of love I've ever shared with strangers.

I looked around. Jennifer was crying. She wasn't alone. I was in tears with her. I'm certain there wasn't a dry eye anywhere with the song, the emotions of love, and being in such a sacred moment.

Kim snapped a photo of the girls singing.

"Your faith was strong, but you needed proof," the girls sang.

I identified with that line in a new and personal way. I began to think about my pilgrimage and the pilgrim walking to Rome and then Jerusalem. And again I considered the Sisters of the Sacred Heart:

Blessed are you, pilgrim, if you discover that one step back to help another is more valuable than a hundred forward without seeing what is at your side.

Appropriate, I thought, since I felt as if I was no longer seeing what was at my side, my travels and experiences blurring into one. I recognized that there was a chance to help another: the pilgrim and his dog. He had a burden, and when the singing was over, I returned to the streets to seek him out.

I found the pilgrim walking up the street from the campground. During our conversation, with me speaking in Spanish and some in English, he told me no one would let him stay the night. The albergues were full. "*Completo*" he said. And the campground would not take his dog. So for tonight, he was sleeping on the portico of the church.

Perhaps it was because I missed Zinger, but I would have carried extra water for the dog if we had been walking together. I would have carried part of their pack had he asked, but he was headed east to Rome, and I west to Santiago. I offered the pilgrim some money, which he refused. I insisted, "*Para usted y su perro?*" For you and your dog?

"*Solimente el perro*" — "only the dog," he replied.

Jennifer and Karen had found dinner and invited Sandra and me to share it. Several younger pilgrims were laughing and having fun and loud conversation filled with inside jokes, memories and exaggerated stories. After dinner, we attended the Pilgrim Mass as a group.

At the end of the mass, the priest called a list of countries by memory, and pilgrims raised their hands as he called out their homeland. Then he offered a blessing and an anointing for each pilgrim. The sisters gave us each a hand-colored star representing the light, life, and love. It echoed the beatitude shared by the Sisters of the Sacred Heart:

Blessed are you, pilgrim, if you search for the truth and make the Camino a life and of your life a way in search of the one who is the Way, the Truth, and the Life.

In that moment, after this day and all the other days before it, I felt my home in the church growing. This was where I was meant to be. We were all standing near the altar, and when I turned around, behind the crowd was the Rome-bound pilgrim, holding his laminated sign. He saw me, smiled, and held up his sign. Another pilgrim hugged him, and as I walked over to him, we embraced,

The pilgrim's voice was clear and strong, and during our hug, in clear English, he said to me, "Buen Camino, I love you."

I don't know that I can explain it other than to say it was the sharing of the Holy Spirit between everyone in the church, between the Rome pilgrim, the others, and me. This is the right place to stay, for the night and for another day.

In the morning, even though I was staying in town, the rules of the albergue were clear: I needed to pack and leave. I sat with the sisters in the church during their morning prayers and songs. I was the lone pilgrim sitting on the wooden pews in the stone church. I said a prayer for each of you and then my pilgrim friends. I said a prayer of gratitude and of safety for the Rome pilgrim and his dog.

Sandra is continuing on. I told her, as I told David and his family, and Peter, John, and John, and Frank and Helen on other days, "I'll see you down the road." It's a promise I feel I can make as we all share a connection in this Camino. There are some connections that seem like they will continue and some people I will not see again. I haven't seen Dan and Maria, nor have I seen Dave and Pam from the early days. Kevin from Chicago is somewhere on the trail as is the fast-walking Maxim. But I feel the connection with the Canadians, with the California family, with Sandra, with all my dinner companions from Burgos.

And that's my story. So many people gave of themselves today—the sketch artist, the singing girls, the Rome-bound pilgrim, and all the pilgrims along the trail.

Giving of yourself is sacred.

Love,

Dad

DAY SEVENTEEN:

"It isn't complicated"

Terradillos de los Templarios, October 7

Dear Chase, Noah, and Cara,

My second day in Carrión de los Condes is a Sunday and my first day not walking. It was harder to rest today than I anticipated. If the laws of physics apply to the human, then a body in motion tends to stay in motion. I spent the midday at a patio table on the corner of the plaza. I chatted with a South African pilgrim who is walking to Santiago, then flying to Barcelona to catch a cruise ship to the United States to see Miami, Las Vegas, and New York before returning to South Africa. His travel companions take photos and promise to send them to Flickr.

Hans arrived later in the day. Peter, John, and John arrived, surprising me because I thought they were a day or two ahead of me. They had kept on walking when I stopped in Ventosa. Late in the afternoon, we all sang with the sisters. This time, the teenage girls were not there, and no one sang "Hallelujah." They day before had been special. The Pilgrim Mass included the same roll call of countries with new and different homelands, and the blessing and star were gifts.

I met Hans from Germany a few days back, but I don't recall in which town. Sandra had mentioned him and had asked her friend Noél about his progress. Hans and I decided on a late dinner, and at the end of the mass, we set out to find a restaurant. Hans is taller than me with a smooth shaved head and modern dark-framed glasses.

An older woman approached us in the plaza and, in Spanish, asked if the mass had ended.

"Yes," we replied.

"*Ven comigo* [come with me]," she commanded. We followed. I expected the reason she had sought out two tall pilgrims was that she had furniture to move from the second floor to the third floor, and in exchange she would give us something to eat. Instead, she turned down a corner and pointed to the Restaurante El Resbalón at the end of the street. Hans seems to have a background in the restaurant business, or maybe he just enjoys them, but he was quick to try several foods and chatted with the restaurant waitstaff and other diners in English and German.

After dinner and sleep, I was on the road again today (Monday).

Halfway is halfway, right? So somewhere along this stretch of days is the halfway point of the Camino. This is my seventeenth day walking, and if thirty-three days gets us to Santiago, we're about halfway. Or not. Terradillos is the halfway point between Saint Jean and Santiago, and it is my stop tonight. Sahagún, a town thirteen or so kilometers farther, has an arch marking the halfway point between Roncesvalles and Santiago. But tonight's stop along the way is at a modern albergue on the west edge of Terradillos de los Templarios.

The one-floor layout is nice, and they have a smart marketing approach: the bigger the room and the more bunkmates you have, the lower the cost. I bunk up with a group of Italian bicyclists.

The laundry and drying lines are at the back of the property, catching both the afternoon sun and a bit of a breeze. The sleeping rooms are at the back as well. Up front is a large yard with tables, a covered porch with seating and tables, and an inside bar and restaurant.

It was in a back hallway between wings of dorm rooms that I found a secret nirvana. It sounds silly, I'm sure, but there were two comfortable chairs. Every other chair I've seen so far on the Camino has been a table chair, no easy chairs or sofas. I felt a bit guilty and antisocial as I sat there alone, but it was one of the first lounging chairs I've sat in during my overnights. I had an awesome short nap before I walked outside to mingle and eavesdrop on the pilgrim stories of the day.

Sometime after I took my shower, John, Peter, and John and their wives arrived, as did two sisters-in-law from the Dakotas whom I met in Ages. The succession of familiar faces is amazing to me.

I sat with the Canadian couples, and they introduced me to David and Ken. David is a retired banker from Australia with a wicked sense of humor, and Ken is a Scotsman, just as quick with a joke. Their geographically opposite English accents made the conversation even funnier.

Ken told the story of being taken off his flight from Australia by the security authorities and seeing his backpack on the tarmac, the only bag on a baggage cart. As he told the story—I have no idea what is true and what is exaggeration—he described putting on a flak jacket and being told that his bag was "vibrating." They wanted him to open it and show the authorities what was in the bag. David nodded, knowing what it was, and then Ken proceeded to tell them it was his battery-operated toothbrush. He ended with a punch line he used throughout his storytelling, "Sure, blame the bankers," he said of his former occupation. The punch line got funnier every time he said it.

Who cares if it was a true story or not? It was entertaining, and Ken's delivery was terrific.

While I know many of the people here, I also know that I will probably walk alone tomorrow. I walked alone today. But as I think about my experience in Zabaldika and then again in Carrión de los Condes, I feel a deep sense of calm and quiet. Being with good people, walking every day, dining on simple meals—it isn't complicated. Most of the complications in my life are complications I create.

Love,

Dad

DAY EIGHTEEN:

"Technology isn't the time waster; it's getting it to work that's the problem"

Sahagún, October 8

Dear Chase, Noah, and Cara,

On this morning's walk, I met Eva, a musician, as she walked out of the other albergue in Terradillos and into the early morning light. We struck up a conversation. She offered me a cookie, which was a good thing since I had run out of Choco Princes, the addictive cookie Sandra introduced me to.

Eva and I had the pilgrim conversation until we met Hans, who had gone farther the night before and stayed in an albergue with only one other pilgrim.

The three of us walked together, stopped for a brief coffee, and walked on to Sahagún. Just outside of town, the arches marking the official halfway point I mentioned in my last letter were bathed in the warm morning light. John and John were posing for and taking photos. We walked through a manicured city park and then into the town.

On the corner was an English-style pub, a good place to stop for the second coffee of the morning and a sweet. I'm making today a short walk day, then heading out in the morning for Mansilla, walking a long, isolated Roman road. The guidebook says it's the oldest stretch of Roman Road in Spain, and I think it is best to do it rested and in one concentrated walk. There are several options and alternative tracks, and by staying today in Sahagún, I've shuffled the breaks as prescribed in the guidebook. I'll combine a day and a half into one long thirty-seven-kilometer (twenty-three-mile) day. I haven't been keeping a daily tally of distance or time. I do some checking, now and then, just to get a rough idea of how long or how far it is between cafés, but clearly tomorrow will be a power day.

The pilgrims came and went from the pub in Sahagún, both familiar faces and new faces. As I left to scout out the albergue, I saw Hans's walking stick resting near the door to a bakery, and I heard him call to me, insisting I taste the pastry. He had managed to walk a block before discovering the best food in the city. After the dinner in Carrión and now this bakery, I think of Hans's walking stick as a pseudo Michelin star for Camino food.

While exploring Sahagún, I walked to the top of the hill overlooking the town to visit a restored monastery, the Monasterio de la Peregrina. In the monastery, I was greeted by a young woman working at a computer behind a lobby desk. I gave her my name, and she told me to pick up my compostela when I was finished touring the museum.

I walked through a glass door and into a large room, a renovated museum hall with old stone, drywall, and display cases. A glass case holding centuries-old texts was against a glass wall, and beyond, I could clearly see the reception desk and the woman's computer screen displaying Facebook. The scene was a classic juxtaposition of communication, from generations ago to today.

Technology on the Camino has been hit and miss. With the surge in phones and tablets, and the availability of Wi-Fi (*Wee-Fee*, as the Europeans pronounce it) is common, and the pay-for-use Internet Café machines sometimes work and sometimes they don't. I had the brilliant idea of showing some photos from Facebook with pilgrims looking over my shoulder in Ages. I bought fifteen minutes of time. It took eight minutes for the computer to boot into Windows XP and another four to open my Facebook profile. In the remaining three minutes, I displayed three photos from a photo album.

None of this is a rant or complaint. In some ways, it was a gift to be able to connect at all, but it reminded me that I have spent an inordinate amount of time in my life getting technology to do what it is supposed to do than actually using it.

I think if I had had the choice, if I had wanted to bring a device with me, I would have brought a small tablet with e-reader software and a Google account. Over Wi-Fi, I could make calls to the states and read text messages. But I am equally glad I did not bring a device and am willing to seek out the occasional relic of an Internet café.

At the end of my self-guided tour of the monastery, the young woman presented me with my first compostela, a colorful document proclaiming my arrival at the halfway point of the Camino. It was numbered 552.

The albergue in Sahagún has two Internet kiosk computers, both not working. And a pay phone. I use the pay phone to confirm my return airline reservations. Now that I am eighteen days into the hike, I'm confident I can be in Santiago to catch a connecting flight to Paris and then home.

So while I muse about technology working or not working and the freedom of being free of the viewfinder, I sit at a table with a pilgrim whom I have seen behind a viewfinder every time I have found him. At the moment, he is studying his iPad, looking at hundreds of photographs, and I'm guessing most are from today. I know the expression on his face. I've been in a similar posture, hunched over a laptop, reviewing the day's take, seeking the right story to tell, and looking at what I had missed.

I'm not comfortable describing myself as a world traveler, but while you three kids have been alive, I've traveled some. Seventeen (now nineteen) counties, and in a dozen of those, I did documentary photojournalism. I spent much of my time in Vietnam, Venezuela, Ecuador, Romania, and Norway behind the viewfinder of still and video cameras.

Early in my planning for hiking the Camino, I made the decision: No cameras. No cell phone. No tablet. I would make notes and reminders but specifically wanted to stay in the moment rather than step outside and reflect, edit, arrange, or compile.

Don't get my abandonment of real-time story making as condemnation. Truly, of the many trips I've been on, this foot-based trek across one of the most beautiful rural landscapes in the world is the ideal trip for a camera. And all the gear. And a full video kit. I saw many pilgrims doing just that and, judging from the glee expressed on their faces, having the most amazing trip of their life. Likewise, the portability of technology, GPS, and Wi-Fi make a tablet or phone the perfect travel companion—small, lightweight, rechargeable. But I chose for me to leave them all behind.

If early pilgrims were dependent on the kindness of strangers for food and water and shelter, I am a techno-pilgrim, dependent on others for photos, communication home, even the time of day. I'm thinking of the many people who took my photo and posted it to Flickr for you all.

Alice from the Netherlands, who took my photo in Logroño and who restores gypsy wagons and then rents them to people to take on vacation is here. She offers to share a cup of tea with me.

Over tea and watching the pilgrim perform his daily photo edit, I reach for the yellow journal and jot down, "Technology is not the time waster; it's getting it to actually work that is the problem."

Love,

Dad

Every Step is a Gift

DAY NINETEEN:

"Even on power days, take time to go slow"
Mansilla de las Mulas, October 9

Dear Chase, Noah, and Cara,

I can't describe the beauty of rural Spain. What has happened to me is that after several days, seeing everything as new has evolved to seeing more detail. The plains of the Meseta have more grandness and open spaces than the tighter forests of earlier days near Ages or the mountains of Saint Jean and Roncesvalles.

On a good day's walk, my body, backpack, shoes, and feet work so well together that they become silent and forgotten. Today was one of those days, and the solitude of my walk reminded me of a quotation I read about musicians and piano players. It is attributed to many musicians and I can't identify who said it first, but the idea is that one musician plays the notes pretty much the same as the next musician. It's the spaces in between the notes that make the music. To apply that to the Camino, it is probably the thoughts in between the steps that make the pilgrimage.

By the time I got to the end of today's hike, I appreciated that my mind was meditatively empty. No worries about worldly problems or concerns, no self-appreciation or self-doubt, no writing and rewriting passages of *Kolby Rae*—just a quiet calm.

Walking alone, I had no one to gauge my pace and no idea of time or place. On the final few kilometers, I saw a solo pilgrim walking on the path along the road between Reliegos and Mansilla de las Mulas. As I walked up to her, I quickly realized how dramatically different our walking pace was. I slowed to almost half my stride, and we talked for five to ten minutes, walking at her slower pace before she stopped for a break and I returned to my earlier pace of the day. The break helped me reset and return back from my meditation, which is good. I needed to be aware of the cars and traffic as I walked into town along the roadway. In the journal, my note reads, "Even on the power days, take time to go slow."

Before dinner in the albergue, I walked further into town and was greeted by Peter, John, and John along with Ken and David from Terradillos around a table. Ken and David were laughing and telling stories. Ken, in Scottish brogue, was relaying a conversation he had with a friend describing the Camino days.

The friend told Ken, "So what you're really telling me, Ken, is that you are on the world's longest pub crawl."

We all laughed, and I remember Noah, when I told him about the Camino, saying, "So what you're telling me is you're going to backpack across Europe."

As Ken told his story, a pilgrim with black-framed Ray-Bans walked out of the bar with a bottle of champagne and three long-stem glasses and crossed the street. It was a scene that looked like it was from a movie poster or a fragrance ad in a magazine. Everyone at the table raised a glass and toasted him as he disappeared inside the municipal albergue.

There are three kinds of albergue ownership or operation. When I say municipal, I mean it is operated by the city government or the local authority. The parochial or religious albergues are run by the local church, and the third category is private albergues run by local business owners. Some of the private albergues belong to an association that sets some standards and does some marketing on their behalf. In a broad sense, the private albergues cost a bit more than the others, maybe one to four euros more per bed. While the others are at the municipal albergue tonight, I am in a private one, the El Jardin del Camino.

This evening, as the pilgrims gathered in anticipation of dinner, it was an unusual scene: a man in his seventies took out his harmonica and played, much to the pleasure and amusement of the younger man with the movie star Ray-Bans. The man had left his champagne and companions and was now switching his attention between his iPhone and his pipe. An older man, drunk, blurted out obscene phrases and fell from his chair, twice. Each time, a pilgrim and one of the employees came to his side and set him back in the chair.

The waitress seated me at a table alone. I looked up to see Jacques and Ivan invite me over. They are French. I had heard them tell their story in Carrión, that as college students, they had decided to hike the Camino together, and now as retirees, they were doing it. Jacques has the better English of the two, and I felt bad for not knowing more French. But we talked about Iowa and Des Moines.

Jacques has an iPhone, and the French version of Wikipedia told him about Iowa (not Ohio or Idaho) and Des Moines. Jacques told me that Des Moines translates to "the Monks."

We talked about France, and I asked them to tell me what part of France I should visit. Pays de la Loire, Charentes, and Aquitaine. They told me stories in English, and I understood most of them. I'm not sure how many of my stories they understood in return, but the literal meaning was secondary to the story-sharing using emotion, body language, and expression. We passed the evening quickly.

As I look back over my notes and think about my letters to you, I am sure you are beginning to think all I do is walk, drink coffee, eat, and sleep. Well, yes, that's about it, except that each time I come to a church and it is open, I step inside, kneel at a pew, and say a prayer for you and for my Camino friends. The church in Mansilla was closed, so I said the prayer as I walked the streets a final time before going to bed.

Love,

Dad

DAY TWENTY:

"In a choice of paths, choose the one going up"
Virgen del Camino, October 10

Dear Chase, Noah, and Cara,

Hello from the other Leon.
    This is almost like being at home, only not really. Before I thought about the Camino, I looked at the weather for León every day but only by technological confusion. Two Mile is near the town of Leon in southern Iowa. So when Google servers decoded the IP address of my computer to figure out what weather forecast it should display, it saw that I was near León. The weather widget showed the weather for the best match it could find, León, Spain. So for being halfway around the world, this is almost home.

    The popular guidebook warns that after the long stretch of quiet on the Meseta, the noise and din approaching León might be overwhelming and suggests the option of taking a bus into the city. There are so many options and combinations of travel to allow anyone to experience the Camino. There is clearly a Camino for everyone. I hiked in, grateful the day was rain free compared to the hike into Burgos. Eva and Hans were waiting at the bus stop as I walked by, planning to ride into town. The morning coffee was up ahead on the edge of León.

    I reflect on the logistics of the Way so far. There is so much that could have gone wrong, yet very little did go wrong, and I haven't heard many stories of trouble. The only time I was truly lost and confused, even if only for a few minutes, was in Bayonne before I arrived in Saint Jean. I stepped out of the train station at Bayonne in search of my hotel that was "only fifty meters from the train station." Even in my jet-lagged and late-night stupor from flying from Boston after two flight cancelations and then a high-speed train ride through southern France, how hard could it be to find a hotel fifty meters away?

I looked up and down the street, then looked at the map included on the paper copy of my reservation, then wandered in a circle and another circle and finally a larger circle, unable to find the hotel. To expand my search any wider would have put me on the bridge over the Adour River. In final exasperation, I turned around to see where I had come from and was greeted by the hotel's neon light. It was small and high above the street. Most likely, it was there to be visible from the bridge more than walkers from the train station. I pressed the security buzzer on the door, stumbled through some horrible attempt at French, and was in my room.

The rest of my walking has been mostly trouble free. I pressed on into León, stopping at a corner grocery and found a tube of Choco Prince cookies.

I caught the eye of a woman I had seen along the trail and stopped. We shared a coffee and some incredible sweets. We swapped the usual stories and somehow got on the topic of Bayonne and the train. I told her how stupid I felt wandering in circles trying to find the hotel that was fifty meters from the station.

"I did the same thing," she told me.

"Really?"

"Yes."

At least there were two of us lost and confused in the dark in Bayonne.

Her husband had told her that he was flying in from Australia to meet her in Santiago. A nice welcome for when she arrived.

On the plaza in front of the cathedral, I found Hans, I found Eva, and I found pilgrims and tourists. There was a stuffed Minnie Mouse outside of a store. There are souvenirs, postcards, and trinkets.

The León Cathedral is big and beautiful but quite different from Burgos. In the quiet, I found a small chapel. After lighting a candle for each of you, I said a prayer of thanks for being this far along on the Camino safely, and I asked for the continued safety of all I had met so far. I said their names, more than twenty of them. We are all separated by miles on the Camino yet somehow connected.

The trek out of León includes walking out of the city with traffic and din not unlike the trek in. Before leaving, there is the plaza where the Parador Hotel sits on stately display. David, Sylvia, Sarah, Beth, and Sandra all told me of their plans to stay there, using words such as *bathtub, clean sheets,* and *pillows* to describe the luxury that awaited them.

Somewhere around day four or five, I began to write a rule. The path on the Camino is well marked with fixed signs and spray-painted yellow arrows, but every so often, the path splits with two ways to go: a well-worn path leading across a field or another well-worn path leading up a hill. More times than not, the correct path is uphill.

On the way out of town, I followed Noél and his friends. They were in search a store to buy a portable speaker for their iPods to listen to music as a group. And then up. Up a pedestrian bridge, uphill, a quick right turn, up another hill, walk, and then up a hill again.

It's from here, in the small town of La Virgen del Camino, that I write you on the outskirts of León. From the outside, this albergue resembles a military building, but once inside, it is a spacious and pleasant stay with large bathrooms and showers, and two or three dormitories. I was the first pilgrim in the door, and by night, fewer than ten were sleeping over. Most probably stay in the city of León.

Peter and Kath joined me, and we set out for dinner together.

Love,

Dad

Every Step is a Gift

AFTER THE WINE FOUNTAIN, NEAR VILLAMAYOR DE MONJARDÍN

THE BURGOS CATHEDRAL

I asked pilgrims along The Way to take my photo and email it to a photo sharing website. You can see all the photos in color at www.flickr.com/photos/fritzcamino or scan the QR code below

On the bridge at Hospital de Órbigo

First coffee of the day   Our dinner together in Santiago

DAY TWENTY-ONE:

"There is no time on the Camino, only now"
Hospital de Órbigo, October 11

Dear Chase, Noah, and Cara,

I must have been quite a sight this morning standing on the corner of a street in the dark, fumbling with my light in search of a yellow arrow and the route to Villar de Mazarife. A woman waiting at a bus stop yelled and pointed. I'm guessing if she waits for the bus every morning, she does the same yell and point for the other pilgrims seeking the road to Mazarife. What's funny is that at the first corner, near the edge of Virgen del Camino, the arrow might be difficult to find, but the next one can't be missed. The Camino has two options; one path leads to Villar de Mazarife and the other to Villadangos del Páramo. The asphalt path is spray-painted with signs and arrows pointing in the two directions to the competing towns.

My first coffee stop was in Fresno del Camino. I walked into town midmorning as the last of the pilgrims were loading their backpacks. We chatted, and they were surprised I'd been on the walk an hour and a half already.

"We're late," the woman told me.

Without thinking, I blurted out, "There is no early or late on the Camino; there is only now."

I immediately felt a bit like a pompous neophilosopher, but they both smiled and nodded. I walked inside the albergue for a café solo and to take a short break from hiking.

Most of the walk today was alone again. I know it's not the shortage of pilgrims but my stopping points that have put me off the cycle of layovers. Today is day twenty-one. A long time ago, in the 1950s, a physician researched and published a book about self-image, reporting that it took at least twenty-one days for his patients to get used to a new look, for example, someone who had had a nose job or a limb amputation. He published a self-help book that led others to re-report on his book, and somewhere along the line, we have accepted the myth of it taking twenty-one days to form any new habit. So I won't claim that walking is my new habit, but I will say that after doing this every morning for three weeks, there is a certain comfort and ease to walking each and every day. Now that I've walked twenty-one days, I'm past my second halfway point as well. There are nineteen days of walking left..

I had to stop for a moment as I wrote that last bit. This entire walk, the idea of walking this many days and this distance, was hard to imagine before I began. I accepted it was possible on faith. Now I toss around phrases such as "Nineteen days of walking left" or "It's only eight kilometers until coffee" as if it's a part of everyday life. Well, I guess it is.

Before I got to the small towns today, Mazarife and Hospital de Órbigo, I walked through farmland. At a small wayside with a picnic table and shade, I waved at a tractor as I slung my backpack over my shoulder, and the farmer quickly slowed down to see if I needed help. I waved him on, and he nodded and smiled. And that's been my experience all along the Way—the local neighbors, shopkeepers, and hospitaleros don't show any sign of pilgrim fatigue. The busy season for pilgrims is the summer, and after a full season of thousands of pilgrims from all different countries and with all levels of expectations, I could easily understand if the Spanish people just wanted to take a break and hide from the backpack-toting, scallop-shell-brandishing pilgrims. But they continue to offer help with a pleasant and genuine smile.

True, pilgrims spend money—although not much—and for the bars and albergues, greeting pilgrims is their livelihood. But everyday people have often stopped what they are doing, such as the woman at the bus stop and the farmer on his tractor, and have pointed the way for me.

However, according to history, not everyone on this stretch of the Way has been friendly. I'm staying tonight in Hospital de Órbigo, and the major landmark here is the thirteenth-century bridge built over an old Roman bridge. It was here in 1434 that a knight, scorned by his lover, took up a jousting challenge and defended the bridge against any and all who would fight him. After jousting for thirty days and having his honor restored, he and his comrades continued on to Santiago to give thanks. I guess that is one way to mend a broken heart.

I was standing at the registration desk in the albergue in the middle of an open courtyard when Sandra called my name. She told me the stories of the Parador Hotel in León and caught me up with stories of David, Sylvia, Beth, and Sarah, who also had stayed at the hotel. Later in the day, we were joined by both Hans and Eva. Hans suggested the Restaurante Los Angeles for dinner.

There are certain friends with whom you can pick up a conversation hours, days, or even years later as if no time has passed between phrases. Many of the pilgrims are like this. I hope each of you has friends like that, and if not, I am certain you will meet some. I joke some about "the pilgrim conversation," which is not really a conversation as it is social sharing. But with these pilgrims and others I've included in my letters to you, there is something unique about what we have shared.

Pilgrim is an awkward word. *Friend* isn't exactly the best word, either. I don't know where any of these people live, or their birthday, or what they do for a job. I suppose if I found them on Facebook, I would know more facts—yet in many ways, I think some of us on the Way know each other better than friends. We hold each other's "Camino Heart," to use the phrase shared by the Bolivian pilgrim I met in Ventosa.

Love,

Dad

DAY TWENTY-TWO:

"Give more than you desire, and receive more than you need"
Astorga, October 12

Dear Chase, Noah, and Cara,

There is an oversized backpack at the entrance to a modern store just off the main plaza in Astorga. It's there I spent part of the afternoon pre-siesta looking through a sporting goods store. I bought two things: a small camera pouch that slides on a belt and an infinity scarf. I almost bought a keffiyeh, or shemagh-style scarf, before I left, but I didn't find one I liked. The infinity scarf will do the same thing and keep me warm when we climb through the final high points of the Way later next week.

If there is one thing missing on my backpack, it's pockets, of any size. It didn't matter so much in the early days of the walk because of the extra cargo pockets on my pants. But my oldest pair of pants has holes growing in both cargo pockets, so now I have a place to keep my glasses if I take them off and an easy way to carry money. Euros come in coins, and I constantly have a pocketful of coins.

Many of the retail stores are open, and there are lots of chocolate shops. Not only are there flavored chocolate candies but also different colors of chocolate: pink, orange, and all shades of brown and dark chocolate. There is a palace designed by Gaudi, a church that is magnificent. Both are closed, so Astorga will be a look-from-the-outside

Every Step is a Gift

kind of visit. Today is a national holiday in Spain, so the television screens are showing images of parades and formal ceremonies.

There is a big central plaza here, as in many of the towns. At the top of the hour, a large clock chimes, and animated figures dressed in a traditional style of maragatos strike the bell at the top of each hour to the applause and smiles of the tourists below.

In the plaza, Sandra discovered a tapas restaurant and was bringing tapas from inside out to her table. Hans had met a local who told him of a restaurant where we should eat. It sounded expensive. Hans said the chef trained under or with Paul Bocuse, and now this restaurant is well known.

On the way down the stairs of the albergue, I looked down and found two twenty-euro bills, nearly fifty-five dollars, on the step. I looked around to point it out to whoever had dropped it, but there was no one nearby. If I hadn't put my own money in the new travel pouch, I would have guessed they were my bills that had fallen through the holes in my pockets. While the money would have paid my share at dinner and despite my quick memory of Matthew 7:7 — "Ask and it shall be given onto you" — the money belonged to another pilgrim. So I took it inside to the volunteer at the front desk. Each of the volunteers I've met at this desk have had different home countries and different home languages. I explained the found money, and she was willing to set it aside for its owner to claim. And if not, it will go to the operation of the albergue.

Hans made 8:00 p.m. reservations at the restaurant. We were seated at the first table. We were alone in the restaurant because the traditional Spanish supper crowd arrives much later. It was the nicest restaurant I've been in on the Camino and perhaps in a year or more. There were no house wines in plain glass carafes; instead, better local varietals were served. Frank would appreciate these wines, I'm certain. The three of us enjoyed them after a toast. *Proost*. We sampled the *pulpo* (octopus) duck, beef, and desserts. Sandra and Hans conversed in German most of the dinner. I could follow their stories, mostly because I've heard them in English, and by now, I know both of their personalities well.

Most of the afternoon, Hans and I were talking about moving to Spain, opening an albergue, and running it in our retirement. The good food and wine only encouraged us to dream more, and the memory of a *se vende* (for sale) sign on a building in the corner of the plaza pushed us to further imaginative dreams.

"A Rock 'n' Roll Albergue," I told them. "Photos of Marilyn Monroe, James Dean, and contemporary movie stars."

We walked by the building after dinner. Sadly, it was not the building that is for sale but an upstairs office above the bank. So the shortest-lived dream of opening an albergue ended on the sidewalks on Astorga.

The idea has stayed with me, not because I truly want to run an albergue, but because it might make an amusing novel. Two expatriates, one American and one German, are forced into an unlikely partnership due to some circumstance. One runs the kitchen; one runs the front of house. I've titled it the *American Rock 'n' Roll Albergue*.

While the town of Astorga has its rich history and Gaudi design, there was a little cantina on the walk into Astorga this morning that offered a different and simple richness. After I left yesterday's town of Óbrigo and passed through two small hamlets, there was a two-hour hike through quiet woodlands and rolling hills that opened onto a flat pasture. In the middle was a single farm building, and in front was a simple food cart and a sign, *Donativo*. The host, David, greeted pilgrims, pointing out the breads, fruit drinks, and spreads. Seeing me, he added, "And for the American, we have peanut butter."

Sandra and Hans conversed in German; we sampled the octopus, duck, beef, and desserts

There were a dozen pilgrims enjoying snacks and chatting. David had two hammocks outside his building and a large machine shed, and the tai-chi-learning young couple I last saw in Ventosa were staying there a few days.

A pilgrim walked off, heading east instead of west, and when David saw her, he rang a ship's bell he has mounted to his cart to catch her attention. He yelled, "*A Santiago!*" and pointed to the west, but she did not respond. He smiled. Clearly this had happened before.

As pilgrims left, David hugged most of us, and when it was my turn to walk on, he said to me, "Have a good life."

My journal note reads, "Give more than you desire, and receive more than you need." The pilgrims with me on this journey have given me more than I can ever return.

Love,

Dad

DAY TWENTY-THREE:

"Push further than you think you can push"
Foncebadón, October 13

Dear Chase, Noah, and Cara,

At the end of today, I jotted, "Push further than you think you can push" in my journal. My note seems to be the opposite of the quotation in the guidebook for today, "Distrust yourself, and sleep before you fight; 'tis not too late tomorrow to be brave."

The Cruz de Ferro is on tomorrow's route. It's an uphill climb from last night in Astorga, and many pilgrims stop in Rabanal del Camino after climbing one hundred meters. Most plan to. That means then hiking a few hours to see the cross. I would like to see it at sunrise.

Even though I am tired, I looked ahead to see Peter and Kath were pushing on, and Sandra was pushing on. I still felt like I had some walk left in me, so I pushed on, too.

The final hill into Foncebadón, the next town, is steep. It's five kilometers and two hundred meters of climb, and once across the road near the top of the trail, our reward is a spectacular view of the valley behind us. We were all winded, even after twenty-three days and over three hundred miles. It was a tough climb.

The albergue is nice, but the bunk beds are in the basement. I did laundry and hung it to dry. Within minutes it began to rain, so I retreated with damp clothes to the small bar, joining a small group of pilgrims enjoying Kas Limon, coffee, wine, and beer. There was a Scottish couple, easily recognizable from the trail. He carried both their gear in a pull cart with handles that were also clipped to his belt. I can't fathom how he pulled the cart up today's hill or down the hill after Alto del Perdón on day four. Pulling uphill has to be unreal, coming down even more of a rush, holding back the weight.

The bartender discouraged us from hanging wet clothes near his radiator to dry them, so we all did what we could to find a clear space near the bunk beds to let them air out.

In the metaphor of life, if the flat Meseta is midlife, these next ten days represent some new physical challenges, perhaps reflective of the later years in life, with steeper climbs and entering the province of Galicia, where the guidebooks and pilgrims say there is much more rain. There are some altitude milestones to take account of. Sorry, no bad dad puns here about the ups and downs of life. By comparison, the first day climb through the Pyrenees reached 1,450 meters, almost a mile high. La Cruz de Ferro on tomorrow's trail is at 1,505 meters, and the highest point on the Camino is just a bit farther down the road at Punta Alta, 1,515 meters.

O Cebreiro, in about three days, is not as high, only 1,310 meters, but that day's climb is the steepest. It begins in Villafranca del Bierzo at 530 meters, and the last five kilometers of the linear walk are nearly 600 meters of climb. The lowest altitude of the walk will be the sea-level towns of Fisterra, Muxía, and Cee, which I will see after Santiago.

Today's gift was walking the extra distance and climb to be present at the Cruz de Ferro at sunrise. After dinner, I took some time to write a while and reflect on the meaning of the Cruz de Ferro tomorrow morning. It has become a shrine of sorts, a collecting point for small stones and tokens of love to be shared with fellow pilgrims to help each understand the purpose of their Camino.

In the bottom of my backpack is a small rock from the end of the dirt road that borders Two Mile on the south. Each day before I left, Zinger and I would walk the half-mile road and return. Zinger looked forward to doing dog things and chasing any cows who had escaped from their pasture. For me, each morning walk was the beginning of each new day, and the Cruz tomorrow marks a beginning of a new day, a new life, a new chapter.

I chose the rock from the end of the road, put in the pack, and tomorrow, I will leave it behind.

A reconciliation.

Love,

Dad

DAY TWENTY-FOUR:

"The only game in town may be the best one"
Ponferrada, October 14

Dear Chase, Noah, and Cara,

Last night, I wrote another letter. It took up four pages in the yellow Rite in the Rain journal. I tore the pages free and have tucked them away. It is a letter I have written to your mom, and I will give her the pages when I fly back.

Your mom and your dad, if you haven't figured out, can be odd human beings. I know there are things about my life and about your mom's life and our life together that are difficult to understand. This isn't the time or the place or the way for us to have a conversation about our choices. The specifics are something between your mom and me; our struggles are our own. I know at times you three have paid the price for our faults. Writing that letter and being at the Cruz this morning was freeing.

There were lots of things left behind at the Cruz. Notes, photos, an ID badge from a job, rocks, stones, jewelry. I left my rock from the end of the dirt road, said a few prayers for each of you, and mom, too. And while reconciliation doesn't erase the past, it's been a long time coming and maybe it's a place to start fresh. Only time will tell.

A tour bus pulled into the parking lot, other pilgrims came down the trail. It was time to hike on and for others to mark their visit. I hope for them they find what they seek. Even if they don't know what it is. I know I have.

Today's hike to the Cruz in the dark and then to the higher points was cold. I had my jacket and enough layers to be warm, and even had my photo taken in Manjarin, just to prove I wore the coat on the trip. but as the trail dropped back down to lower levels, I was happy to be warm enough to shed the coat once I walked lower to Acebo and Riego de Ambros.

To be totally honest, I don't remember much of today's walk. I think after leaving the rock, and some of the feelings, regrets, disappointments, anger, and sadness the rock represented, my mind was pretty empty. I felt released, and after warming a little bit, had a great day. The resting point suggested in the guidebook, Molinaseca, is a pretty town with several inviting albergues on the other side of a walk across an old roman bridge. But I was still energized by the forgivness this morning at the Cruz and still had plenty of daylight left, so I walked on to Ponferrada, taking the longer scenic path into the city. The guidebook only lists one albergue in town, so I ask at a tourist information shop and was told there is only one.

Despite being behind Hans, Sandra, and others on the pilgrim trail, I somehow manage to be one of the first to the albergue. Either taking the long way around, or not stopping as often for coffee has put me back in the early arriving group. It's a big place, the only place, in town. Up the road, the Knights Templar castle has a tourist hotel or two nearby, and there is likely a few casa rurals, but this is the only albergue in town. There is a very small chapel in the compound and this chapel offered a quiet respite. On the kneeler, I the list of names I pray for has grown even longer. With each day and each stay, there are more pilgrims I remember and pray for their safety, their continued good health, and protection from injury.

I lit a candle for each of you, which to be honest, wasn't really a candle at all. There are small coin operated collections of LED's under a plexiglas cover to represent candles. It makes money for the parish and prevents the soot and smoke staining caused by real candles. It prevents a few fires, too.

I guess you are as surprised as I am I've been in chapels and on kneelers more in the last twenty-four days than in the last twenty-four months. Each time I kneel, I am covered with both a sense of calm and purpose.

Tonight's dinner was pizza because many of the restaurants are either closed, or opening later than pilgrim time, It is a nice change of pace from the traditional pilgrim's meal.

Chase, as a side note, I brought the nice custom-made leather belt you gave to me as my belt for the trip. Tonight I noticed I was wearing it one notch tighter than normal. It seems that not only did I leave some emotional past behind at the Cruz de Fero, I seem to be leaving some extra pounds along The Way, too.

Love,

Dad

DAY TWENTY-FIVE:

"A true pilgrim helps another"

Villafranca, October 15

Dear Chase, Noah, and Cara,

It rained off and on during this morning's walk for coffee and off and on most of the day. Sandra reminded me, "There is no bad weather, only wrong clothes." In her German accent, she said, "Clothes-es." I smiled.

By the time we got to Columbrianos, I was ready to have a coffee and rest. There was a narrow but sufficient red and white awning over tables sitting in a small alley at the Cafe Bar Gran Sol, and as I sipped my café solo pequeño, I struck up a conversation with a pilgrim I had seen off and on the last couple of days. He told me his story of the Camino.

"Every day I walk, I think of one year of my life. Today is day twenty-four. I had some bad times when I was twenty-four, and today, it is raining. For two years, I lived in the Rocky Mountains in the United States, and I was on the highest point of the Camino yesterday. All things are connected."

It struck me as an interesting way to reflect on a life along the Way. Someone in his or her twenties or thirties might reflect on a few years. At age fifty-three, I could begin my reflection after I turned twenty, the year my dad died. I could reflect on a year for each day between

Saint Jean and Santiago. The metaphor for life would have been my personal retrospective. Since this is day twenty-five, adding twenty-five to age twenty would make today's day about the year I turned forty-five, which is the year we bought Two Mile Ranch.

In the stopover town of Villafranca, Hans had scouted the restaurants, and we were sitting inside one having another good meal. At another table sat a pilgrim who does not speak. Not only is he on a silent pilgrimage, but he is also deaf. He sat alone, showed the waitress a sign that I think explained his silence and inability to hear, and then pointed on the menu.

Each of us commented on both his bravery and the difficulty making this pilgrimage would have. However, it's just another language barrier, and the Spanish have been very accommodating and patient with each of our limitations. Then the pilgrim sitting with us asked wryly, "If he's doing a silent retreat, does that mean he doesn't snore?"

If he's doing a silent retreat, does that mean he doesn't snore?

We all glanced over, thinking he could be the ideal bunkmate.

Later that night in the albergue, I used the Internet. The computer is in a room that was built into the rock hill behind the albergue. The rock is part of the room. Spanish keyboards use a slightly different key arrangement than the ones in the United States. The pilgrim on his silent retreat pointed to the computer keyboard, gestured the "@" sign, and showed me the key combination to use to include it as part of an email address. I was grateful for his kindness.

Depending on which guidebook you read, there are three paths out of Villafranca. The one along the asphalt road is a definite no for Hans, Sandra, and me. That leaves the trail called the Dragonte and the one called the Enduro. The Dragonte is described in much detail in Jack Hyatt's book about the Camino. The Enduro is described in the German guidebook, and Sandra chose that one. Hans, too, was heading out on that one.

I was leaning toward the Dragonte, hills and all. But when Sandra and I reached the intersection where the three Camino routes diverge, I looked around. We had ruled out the flat asphalt. To my left was the Dragonte, down a deceptively flat road. To my right was the route to the Enduro on a road leading up.

"*Camino* means *up*," Sandra said with a grin both making fun of and agreeing with my adapted definition.

I took a deep breath, and up the hill we walked. We went about three kilometers when we came to a scenic overlook. When we stopped, my glasses fogged over, and I took them off.

Before I had left on the Camino, I had an eye exam and received a new prescription, but realizing I would be hiking for forty days, I elected to wait until my return to get the new frames and lenses. This made the glasses I was wearing a touch more disposable if I were to break them. But as a rule, I don't break my glasses often.

We walked farther down the trail, and after walking a few kilometers, I realized I was not wearing my glasses. I felt the pouch, where I was now keeping my glasses when I took them off, and then the pocket with the hole in my cargo pants. No glasses.

Out of earlier habit, I had put them in my pocket just for a little bit, and my best guess is they had fallen out somewhere back on the trail. The most logical place was between the lookout and where I was standing. I called ahead to Sandra, who stopped on the trail and turned around.

"I need to go back. I'll see you down the way."

"See you," she replied with a confident smile and continued on.

This was the first time I had walked against the flow of pilgrims. As I met each pilgrim, I asked if they had seen a pair of eyeglasses and pantomimed eyewear. Each said no.

I met Hans, who said the only sensible reaction in German, *Scheisse*. He quickly turned and walked back with me along the way.

We met pilgrims, who were startled to see the two of us walking the opposite direction. A single, a pair, a trio, and then as we approached the scenic lookout, I was confident the glasses would be there.

We looked around on the ground and in the grass, and neither of us saw them. A pair of women approached from the rail, and we asked them.

One of them exclaimed, "There!" And underneath my foot were my glasses, with one temple broken free. Found because of Saint James, the Camino, God, and pilgrims.

I thought about the pilgrim who had set his backpacking tent on the table to be discovered by Kevin the next day. The farmer walking toward me near a Y fork in the trail who yelled and pointed the correct direction. Hans for walking back, and the girl who exclaimed, "There!" The silent pilgrim with his @ sign pantomime. Maria, who translated with the bank about the ATM. And the beatitude from the Sisters of the Sacred Heart:

> *Blessed are you, pilgrim, if you discover one step back to help another is more valuable than a hundred forward without seeing what is at your side.*

I had stopped to help the Rome pilgrim, and so many more have stopped to help me.

Love,

Dad

DAY TWENTY-SIX:

"Give people and places a second chance"

Ruitelan, October 16

Dear Chase, Noah, and Cara,

During the last twenty-six days, I don't recall meeting anyone I disliked. Some of that must be luck. After all, some people naturally rub each other the wrong way. The snoring from the two-in-the-morning crowd might have kept me awake, but it was hard to pinpoint the sound on any one pilgrim, and by daybreak, all was forgotten or forgiven.

There have been some people I have met along the way for whom I didn't fully appreciate why I had met them. Let me try and explain what I mean.

I have seen more and more by my experiences that I meet people on the Camino for a reason. A shared joke, a new junk food addiction, restaurant recommendations. True, there are casual meetings and conversations that last thirty seconds in a café, and these people are never to be seen again. But the people I have spent time with seemed to be people who continued to appear along the way.

I can say the same about the places. There really hasn't been a bad place anywhere along the Camino, not a bad town. Some pilgrims and guidebooks have spoken harshly of the larger towns of Burgos and León (oddly, not Pamplona). They were nice for big cities, a part of life on the Camino like the Meseta or the towers of haystacks we'd seen in the earlier days. The night in Hornillos was one of the oddest, partially because of the number of flies and the odd lightning storm before going to bed.

But if one town had the oddest feeling on the Camino, it was Ruitelan, the town today. When we arrived in the town, it was mostly deserted. We walked in fine rain and drizzle.

There was something different about the albergue. It was empty. The hospitalero wasn't warm and inviting but wasn't outwardly odd, either. The albergue was clean and affordable. Outside, Hans took a look around, and then he and his walking stick continued on to the next town.

There was no store in town, and the only sign of life was the bar café across the street. The albergue offered a simple meal at a low price. Like the albergue in Ponferrada, it was the only game in town.

Late in the afternoon, I wandered into the bar across the street and found Ken and David. Ken from Scotland was on his second Camino; David from Australia was on his first. Our paths had not crossed since Mansilla. On the television was the Spanish emcee Toñi Moreno and her live show *Entre Todos* on TVE. If I am being honest, she is probably the first media personality I've ever had a crush on. I understood only a few phrases of her show, but the locals in every town are glued to their screens each afternoon to watch it. She has that gift of the screen. Even without a full translation, I understand her appeal.

Ken told a story about a woman he had walked with during the first Camino and how he had invited her along on the second, but she didn't join him. Then he told of an added twist. As he walked the early part of this Camino, he struck up a conversation with another woman from Australia, and as they talked the woman asked, "Are you from Scotland?"

Ken answered, "Yes."

"Is your name Ken?"

Again, he answered, "Yes."

"I have a letter for you."

Ken's friend from the year before had sent it with her, saying, "If you run into Ken from Scotland, please give it to him."

Another example of Saint James providing, the Camino providing, and the interconnected world we all share. No high-tech GPS or tracking numbers. Just the faith of the letter-writing woman who might by chance run into her friend and ask her to deliver a letter to her friend from a country halfway around the world during a five-hundred-mile hike across Spain.

David, quick with a joke and oozing with the confidence of retirement, told funny stories and more personal stories of his life, including the loss of two wives to cancer. He said he wished he had a guitar. I had seen one in the albergue and told him. Sandra came and joined us, and she quickly won Ken's and David's hearts.

We returned to the albergue in time for dinner, a soup and simple pasta around a long communal table.

David plucked and strummed the guitar, leading a sing-along. We all managed to remember half or a little more of each of the songs he played, mostly Beatles and sixties classics. He's quick with chords, and more and more people joined us until the long table covered with white linen was filled from end to end. There was a father–son pair from Denmark; the son said their names were too difficult to pronounce, and instead they came to be known by the trail names of Denmark and Papa Denmark. Sandra, David, and Ken were there. A French man and his hiking companion were there. He had big hair and an even bigger personality, though I never learned his name. He led a singing of "Ultreïa."

Eva appeared near the end of the sing-along and sang a song. Her voice and her style are amazing. Singing is what she is meant to do with her life. It's a rare gift she shared, and I hope she knows it.

I think of my TV crush Toni and her show *Entre Todos*, which translates roughly into "between everyone" or "together." Toñi brings people together every afternoon via her show and compassion. What she does on the screen, we are living around the table in Ruitelan. In her show, her war cry is "*Que Tengo!*" It's a catchphrase meaning, "What do I have?"

To answer tonight, and I guess every night, we have each other.

Love,

Dad

DAY TWENTY-SEVEN:

"It's a family affair"

Fonfría, October 17

Dear Chase, Noah, and Cara,

The quiet sleep in the albergue was stirred softly this morning by music, first the classical "Ave Maria," then *Swan Lake*. The French pilgrim with the big hair stepped out of bed and put his headlamp on. He was wearing only his underwear, and he began to dance as a ballerina. His friend cheered. The rest of us had a good laugh. The hat trick of his performance was ABBA's "Dancing Queen." Trust me, even I can't make this stuff up.

Peter, Kath, Sandra, and I shared a wine in the bar and a piece of Santiago cake—an almond torte. We are in Galicia now, the final state, and the terrain and the building style have all changed. The surroundings are more Celtic than Spanish. Tonight's stop ended up being Fonfría, and for dinner, our group walked down the hill and across the road to a farm building. I'm not sure what it was in a past life, but it's a large open space with a big central fireplace, a kitchen to the right, and an elevated floor that holds a long, arcing table. There were thirty to forty people including the family with five children, who all looked under age of ten. The father had a pushcart with all their gear. If the Scottish couple with the pushcart had had a challenge, this man had multiple challenges. They sat at one end, and Denmark was across from me with Papa Denmark to my side. Peter and Kath were there, chatting with Sandra.

Papa Denmark and I began to talk about farming—the challenges and issues of small-scale production, animal welfare and regulation, earning a living. We shared hobby farming, to put a label on it.

There is something about seating everyone at the same table that changes the mood for the better. Over dinner, Denmark, whose real name is Bjorn but is convinced that is too difficult for others to pronounce, told stories. He's a great storyteller. His father, Morten, whom his son nicknamed Papa Denmark, told me Denmark is a lawyer.

I commented, "What a great gift it is to walk the Camino at age thirty." I wondered what it would be like to walk again when he is his father's age. Denmark was not intrigued by the idea. Papa Denmark smiled and nodded knowingly.

I think as a dad—well, as your dad—it's not my place to tell you how to live your life. I'm not that kind of dad. Neither was my dad, so I guess the acorn doesn't fall far from the tree. And when it comes to making a pilgrimage of any kind, even walking the Camino, I can't say you "should" do it. You can walk a pilgrimage like this only for yourself, not for someone else. But if you do decide to walk the Camino, I hope you will tell me about it. And if you want some company, I'd be glad to come along. I think of the first siblings I met walking the Camino with their parents. I think of David and Sylvia and their daughters, Sarah and Beth, and I think of Papa Denmark and Denmark. I think, too, of the honeymoon couple from Israel, the Scottish pull-cart couple, and the pull-cart family at this table. It's a solo pilgrimage. It's an individual choice. It's a journey of solitude. But if you chose to follow the path and ask me along, I'll gladly join you.

Love,

Dad

DAY TWENTY-EIGHT:

"I've got nothing; sometimes you just need to make it up"
Sarria, October 18

Dear Chase, Noah, and Cara,

When I look over my notes for today and my advice, this is what I wrote: "I've got nothing; sometimes you just need to make it up."
Sorry, that could make this letter a bit short. And if at some point in the future you turn to this letter for advice, here it is: sometimes you just need to make it up.

I don't think my parents had much advice for me. Maybe that's why I'm compelled to write these letters with a daily lesson learned for you to share. On the one hand, my parents were world travelers—Guam, the Philippines, and around the United States—but they were not free spirits. Dad served in the Navy. Your aunts—my sisters—grew up moving from place to place. And as the family of an officer—Dad was lieutenant commander when he retired—the family was cash poor but enjoyed a nice quality of life.

Dad retired when I was three years old, and both your aunts moved out on their own by the time I was age eleven. So while we are of the same family, we grew up in very different times and households. I am used to "making it up" and figuring new things out.

Your aunt Carol Sue gave me the travel bug early. She took me to

Mexico City in my teens and twice to the Yukon. She was supportive of each of my excursions and missions later in life. As I write this, I wish I had traveled more with each of you, but there is time. I look forward to hearing your view of the world you discover.

Today's walk was very nice, and the rain stayed away until the end of the afternoon. Sarria, a small town of thirteen thousand, was my next best hope for an eyeglasses store that could help me fix my frames. But after asking for help in two stores, they looked at the temple and said they could not fix it.

In the backpacking store, they had lots of camping equipment but did not sell CamelBaks. A few days ago, after a short break when leaving Ponferrada, I discovered the end mouthpiece and valve had fallen off of mine or been snagged off as I put on my backpack. The CamelBak worked without it, but if I set the pack at the wrong angle, gravity takes over and spills water on the floor or ground. My hope was that here in this larger town, they would sell the part. But no luck there, either.

So, a bit like my advice, sometimes you just have to make it up.

I have a loose collection of events from today—some new food, some new pilgrims, and a new bunkmate.

At dinner tonight, I ordered a hamburger with everything. Everything includes a fried egg, sunny side up, on top. Outside at a table, three pilgrims, their voices amplified by several beers, were reuniting. One had hiked from Saint Jean; two others had come to join her in Sarria. Sarria is a common starting point for pilgrims who wish to walk the final hundred kilometers (sixty-two miles) and earn their compostela.

Just before going to sleep, the man who was staying in the room pointed to a small, portable CPAP machine to help him breathe because of sleep apnea. He was saying, *"La machina, la machina,"* and then holding his hand over his face, miming a breathing mask and taking deep breaths, sounding a bit like Darth Vader. This could be an interesting and sleepless night.

Love,

Dad

DAY TWENTY-NINE:

"Don't begin until you are ready"

Portomarín, October 19

Dear Chase, Noah, and Cara,

My first thought this morning was the happy realization that the rain had stopped. The tiny bedroom was quiet except for the gentle sound of Darth Vader's CPAP machine. Surprisingly, it was much nicer white noise and less disturbing than snoring. I considered walking with him the rest of the Camino to let his machine be the sound buffer against future snoring pilgrims, but he was still sleeping. The woman in the top bunk was sleeping, too, and the bed beneath me was empty.

I was moving slower than normal. It took me longer to gather my things into my pack and even longer to find my shoes and put them on. I was finally getting ready to head out when the woman from the sleeping room walked down with my towel, asking if it belonged to me. It was a nice touch of pilgrim kindness.

I donned my pack, headed off down the street, and looped through the small stores and shops. Last night, a bike store was open, and they had what the pilgrim backpacking store did not: a replacement valve for my CamelBak in stock. I walked through the older section of town past most of the albergues. I waved at Hans, who was sitting in the lobby of one as I passed by, and then I grabbed breakfast at an open restaurant.

The day had a sleepy feel to it, and I was in no rush. I sat at the bar and ordered. Most of the customers were local, with a handful of pilgrims. A few of the pilgrims' gear was too clean and their clothes too fresh. They've just begun their Camino here. A rough, rainy start. I felt sorry for them.

Today's walk was mostly alone, and I found myself thinking about the beginning and being prepared. Seeing the new pilgrims this morning let me think back to my first days, the night before leaving Saint Jean and then the first morning up the hill into the Pyrenees. Today's hike is flat in comparison to the days behind me. The climb is only two hundred meters.

Early this morning, after about an hour's walk, I came to the town of Barbadelo. On the left side of the road I was greeted by a priest, who was standing at the edge of the wall surrounding the Iglesia de Santiago. Inside the wall, the grey stone church is close, and then beyond it is an open green space. The church inside was cool and damp, and it smelled a bit musty, covered by incense. I rested my backpack against the back wall and knelt in a pew.

I began my prayer with a prayer of thanks for my safety and good health. I said a prayer for you three and began to remember the pilgrims I have met along the Way. I considered the priest whose daily mission was to wait for and greet pilgrims as well as his own local parish. I marveled at the simplicity of purpose in his life and then wondered if we all don't share the same simplicity of purpose, that we only choose to make it more complicated.

I thought about stopping here—in this moment, in this life. I could do this forever, standing by the church wall, greeting pilgrims, granting them solitude on their journey. I'm not sure how long I stayed, but in time, I got up, thanked the priest, and gave a small donation in return for the stamp on my compostela.

On my way across the footpath, around the wall, and then out to the road, I remembered two quotations from Martin Buber. The first is, "All real life is meeting." And then the second: "All journeys have secret destinations of which the traveler is unaware." And here I am, headed for a secret destination, not just Santiago or Fisterra.

The town of Portomarín has become the location for a mini-reunion, and Jennifer has organized a dinner at a central meeting place. Karen, Hans, Sandra, Denmark, Papa Denmark, Eva, and I were all here. The restaurant overlooked the bridge over the man-made lake. When they built the dam and made the lake, they relocated the entire town to the top of the hill, including moving the church, block by block and stone by stone, and reassembling it.

To get to the town, you walk along the sidewalk across that high and long bridge. The winds were brisk today, and I can only imagine the crossing in bad weather. As a final triumph or challenge, there is a set of stone steps to climb to the top of the hill where the relocated town sits, overlooking the valley and lake below. The water level is low enough this time of year to see what remains of the original town.

The shops in the town have more souvenirs and tchotchkes than stores earlier along the Way. León and Burgos had some. I'm only guessing that these things sell better here because we are in the last one hundred kilometers of the Way. There are many more casual tourists and more people meeting or dropping off pilgrims who are walking the distance to Santiago for a compostela. There are patches, trinkets, statues, all kinds of things emblazoned with the yellow arrow or the shell design or images from the trail.

None of the people I have been walking with was interested in carrying more weight — but it helped pass the time to look over the things for sale.

After spending so much of the day in silence, the loud restaurant and conversation is invigorating. In the albergue, one of the pilgrims who has just started his one-hundred-kilometer journey has serious and significant blisters on his feet. I don't know if he will rest or will stop. Perhaps he rushed the first day or two, or perhaps he didn't stop enough.

I am glad that I waited to leave this morning and equally glad to be on the road again tomorrow, fortunate that I have not been held back by injury or pain.

Love,

Dad

DAY THIRTY:

"A warm fire eases the day"

San Xulián, October 20

Dear Chase, Noah, and Cara,

There are just three more nights' sleep before we arrive at the Cathedral de Santiago. There are roughly sixty kilometers left, but the consensus among the group of pilgrims I talk with most is to arrive in Santiago in time for the noon Pilgrim Mass. To do that means making the final day hike into the city a short walking day of only a few hours. So as we talked off and on during the day at our stops, we decided we'll be stopping short of Santiago on the thirty-second day, either in Monte do Gozo or any of the many albergues, which have become more numerous because of the addition of pilgrims who walk only the final one hundred kilometers to receive their compostela. There are many albergues in each town and at the stopping points suggested in the guidebooks.

To avoid the crowds and in keeping with our pattern of dining with the locals, Hans, Eva, Sandra, and I walked on beyond the suggested end of the stage and wandered in San Xulián to discover a small albergue that is more like a casa rural than dorm. The rooms are small.

It was a cool night, and the autumn cool came in the late afternoon. The hospitalero had a very hot fire in the fireplace. The warm, dry heat filled the seating area of the café bar, and we were huddled together. A teacher from Germany began a German language conversation with Hans and Sandra. Eva joined in as well. I was relieved for them all because they have been speaking in English for my benefit most of the day. The teacher mentioned it would be nice to have a salty snack, so I grabbed the partial bag of Corn Nuts I had left in my pack and shared them around the table.

Four of the pilgrims in the café were newcomers to the Way, starting in Sarria. They are college students from Texas in a study abroad program in Italy. They had a few days off and thought walking the Camino would be fun. Hans was an amazing gentleman and forgave their lack of manners when they unceremoniously moved his sleeping bag and clothes off his bed and claimed it for their own.

Four of the pilgrims in the café are newcomers to the Way, starting in Sarria

One of the students is premed and talked to me about his grades, his admissions test scores, and how he hopes they will help him get into a good medical school. I suggested that mentioning he walked the Camino de Santiago might demonstrate some desirable character traits for someone whose life ambition is to care for others. He looked blankly at me. I smiled. In time he will understand. He is here and walking. That's what counts most.

The hospitalero is a storyteller, and his wife is the chef. They offer a wonderful meal on fine china at a cost of only nine euros and in the morning a breakfast for three. I can tell he gives his life to the business. He has a passion for being a good host. I had set my wet clothes on the drying rack he provides to guests, and when I checked again, he had moved the rack out of the shade and into the sun as the sun moved lower in the sky.

Today's photo, if you see it, is kind of funny. As we were sitting outside before the sunset, a local farmer walked his cattle up the street. Even as we approached Santiago and with more and more small towns, the rural life of the village has still been dominant.

I don't miss my camera or regret not bringing one, but the next time

F.R. "Fritz" Nordengren

I take a trip like this, I'll bring it along. There is enough to see and enough time in places to find unique and amazing images. It would be a different trip—and even more so because instead of documenting someone else's travel or mission work, I would be documenting my own.

But for this trip, today's photo of me sitting in the street with the cows and the images from the Alto del Perdón and from the bridge at Hospital de Órbigo will be the memories.

Love,

Dad

DAY THIRTY-ONE:

"We walk by faith"

Arzúa, October 21

Dear Chase, Noah, and Cara,

If there were a music playlist for the Camino, I know a couple of the songs that would be on it. I wrote you about "Me and Bobby McGee" and its hook, "Freedom's just another word for nothin' left to lose." That's on the playlist. Roger Miller's "King of the Road" seems to be a must-play, too. Cohen's "Hallelujah" is in the mix, to be sure, as is the song I am working on for *Kolby Rae*.

Another song, a more obvious choice, came to me as I thought about the distance we have traveled over the Way. Do you remember the Proclaimers? Probably not, but their song "I'm Gonna Be (500 Miles)" with its chorus, "I would walk five hundred miles, and I would walk five hundred more," has been in my head all day.

While light rains have danced with me all along the way, the rains picked up just near Arzúa, the stopping point today, leaving thirty or so kilometers to Monte do Gozo. Tonight's stop is the first high-rise albergue, with several floors of beds. In the summer rush, each floor is full; in October, it's vacant.

Jennifer is there. Karen is with her, and they were making dinner. The rain came down harder, and the walk to the *supermercado* was soggy, but I stayed dry. I'm impressed with the poncho I bought on impulse. The rain stays out, and it breathes pretty well.

Grocery runs now have a shopping list: a loaf of bread, although none compares with French loaves and the loaves from the Basque region; apples; Corn Nuts; a bag of olives; and Choco Prince cookies. I've become a multinational junk food junkie.

As we walked back in the rain and then sat in the common area of the albergue before going to sleep, I thought about the early planning for my walk. The most common question I heard about my decision to walk the Camino was, "Why are you doing this?" It was a fair question considering I am a non-Catholic, a casual Christian with little religious training or indoctrination. Taking a walk of faith struck many of my friends and family as out of the ordinary.

Don, one of my closest friends, asked me what I would do if I was unable to get the time away from my job as a university professor. I told him I would quit and that it would work itself out. He reacted by telling me I had more faith than he did. His reply caught me off guard and made me wonder if my walk was more folly than faith. After all, he is a devoted and confirmed Catholic who summers in the shadow of the Vatican, sharing his love of photojournalism and his tremendous skill in photography with American college students. I took his words to heart and accepted that mine was a walk of faith.

Noah and Cara, I think you were with us at dinner when your mom asked me, "So what's the sound bite if someone asks me why you are doing this? What do I tell them?"

My reply sounds and reads snarky, but it is as honest now writing this as it was in those days before I left: "Tell them, 'If you have to ask, you'll never understand.'"

I looked around the room at the international group of pilgrims. Out of curiosity and not judgment, I wondered what each person sought from our journey. There are probably as many different goals as there are pilgrims. I don't know if this is something you can understand unless you hear the calling. I'm not sure I fully understand what I'm being called for. I found the beatitudes and read this one tonight:

Blessed are you, pilgrim, if your knapsack is emptying of things and your heart does not know where to hang up so many feelings and emotions.

Every Step is a Gift

The Camino, and perhaps life, is too big to fully understand. There is room for mystery, for the unknown. Not everything can be seen, heard, or measured. In Corinthians, there is the passage: "We walk by faith, not by sight."

Love,

Dad

F.R. "Fritz" Nordengren

DAY THIRTY-TWO:

"Don't rush the ending"

Monte do Gozo, October 22

Dear Chase, Noah, and Cara,

The beatitude that goes with what I wrote in my journal for the three of you is this:

Blessed are you, pilgrim, if on the way you meet yourself and gift yourself with time, without rushing, so as not to disregard the image in your heart

On the hill overlooking Santiago is a modern collection of one-story dormitories and supporting buildings. The pope greeted World Youth Day in 1989 dressed as a pilgrim. Historically, the hill is called Mount Joy, for the pilgrim's thrill at seeing the Santiago Cathedral for the first time.

It's only a few kilometers outside of Santiago. It would be easy to continue on, but several of us have stopped here. Others have stopped farther back. I'm sure some continued on and will be dining in Santiago tonight.

The albergue resembles a military barracks. Each room in the long dormitory holds eight people. They have a nice set of closets at each room door, but they create a bit of a bottleneck as people move in and out and try to settle, unpack, and pack again and move on in the morning.

It's rainy and windy, and it's late in the season. The restaurant offers cafeteria-style seating and a limited menu of made-to-order food. The ambiance lacks the homemade touches and pride of the smaller albergues. There are two large dining rooms, and both were closed. But it's easy to imagine the festival midsummer when they are at capacity of eight hundred pilgrims.

It's not a bad place, but it's a reminder: for most, the Camino ends tomorrow. I think those of us here have decided not to rush the ending.

The Frenchman with big hair and his partner are here. He is not dancing ballet. Instead, he looked at me and announced to the room, "I remember you from Ruitelán. You snore all night." He and his partner laughed, and the others in the room gave me a dubious look.

As I write this, I am filled with very mixed feelings. The sense of pride and accomplishment are tempered with regret and sadness. Walking every day has been my purpose the last thirty-two days. Each day, I walked with focus to arrive at night. This day was a big walk, covering twenty kilometers by noon and a total of thirty-five for the day.

Tomorrow's arrival in Santiago is both celebration of the metaphor of life as well as the end of that metaphor. It's a little death. And while I am nowhere close to my physical death, the metaphoric death hits a bit close to home. It's not something we have talked about much.

You never got to know your grandparents, my mom and dad. Truth be said, I never got to know them, either. My mom died when I was thirteen, in 1973. My dad seven years later, just before I turned twenty. As a result, I didn't have a role model for forming an adult relationship with you three. Sure, I remember each of you as infants, toddlers, and young children. I knew you and enjoyed you as children. But it's the people you are becoming who will share the meaningful and memorable times in all of our lives, and likewise your lives with each other.

Even though it was my parent's physical death, it was also the death of my childhood. I had to redefine who I was, and who influenced me. Tomorrow, my arrival in Santiago is a metaphoric little death in this physical portrayal of my life. It will redefine who I am and who influences me.

So how does that relate to you?

If the camino is like life, than it's also true that life is like the Camino. And just like parts of the Camino prepared me for tomorrow's walk into Santiago and the end, life let's us prepare for endings, too.

That's what life is: a balance of holding on and letting go.

When each of you was born, one of the hardest things I had to do was to leave the hospital and not take you with me. It's kind of funny to think about, you were less than a day old, but it was unnatural to think I would leave without you. When you were each old enough to go to a preschool, the parenting advice at the time — and maybe is still given — was to make a clean transition and departure. To drop you off in the safe confines of the room, with a teacher and your friends, and then to turn around a leave, no matter how much you objected or cried. Somehow, I was able to do that, and within minutes you were off to new adventures and at the end of the day, sometimes reluctant to come home.

Chase, it was with that memory that I did one of the other hard things I had to do as your father. Well, it was hard for me, anyway. That was leave you in the dorms at college to begin your life as a scholar. There was no picking you up at the end of the day. It was a long, lonely drive back to Iowa, I mourned the death of your childhood.

Noah and Cara, you will soon have that same day. Each of you have or will have a day when you step out on your own and it will bring the death of your childhood. There is a lesson to share, both for now and the future. As in the beatitude, I hope that when you have metaphoric deaths in life and other changes, you are able to gift yourself with time and not rush the ending so you don't disturb the image in your heart.

Love,

Dad

DAY THIRTY-THREE:

"Santiago, listen for the music"

Santiago de Compostela, October 23

Dear Chase, Noah, and Cara,

The walk into Santiago was in a half-hearted rain. The city streets were busy with an early morning rush. Breakfast was coffee and a chocolate croissant, followed by moving on into the older section of the city, down some narrow streets, and along the north side of the cathedral, under the archway, and into the giant Plaza del Obradoiro.

The plaza was empty of tourists and pilgrims except for a few early risers. Hans and Sandra posed and offered to take each other's and my photo. It was still and quiet. I took a deep breath. It felt more like our morning coffee stop than the end of the journey.

And then I heard it—music coming from the archway on the cathedral's north side. Later on, after spending this day and night in Santiago, I learned that a lone bagpiper played almost around the clock there. But it was not bagpipes; this was a keyboard and violin.

I knew the music. I knew the tune. I was just not sure if I really heard it or if it was the wind or some other trick that sounded like music. I crossed the square and got closer, and the music was clear, sweeter, louder.

It was Cohen's "Hallelujah." It put a lump in my throat. Learning later that the bagpiper normally played the tunes here, I couldn't give an earthly explanation for the timing of the musicians or the song.

On the streets, I ran into Buen Camino, who recommended an albergue. It was new, modern, and nearby. They had lockers to secure a backpack, and it was freeing to walk around the city. At the same time, while everyone around me was finishing his or her pilgrimage, I still had seven more days and two hundred kilometers to walk.

In the pilgrim office, I was greeted, and I answered the questions about my pilgrimage. Where did I begin, and what was the purpose of my pilgrimage? The clear religious purpose and renewed faith filled me. The woman behind the counter wrote my name and explained that because mine was a religious pilgrimage, my name was written in Latin.

She stamped my credential and handed me the compostela. I had done it. I had walked the pilgrimage from Saint-Jean-Pied-du-Port to Santiago as millions of pilgrims had done before me, sharing this sacred Christian road.

Outside, Denmark and Papa Denmark are holding court, taking photos and spreading the news of a dinner and party for everyone who may have crossed paths in the last thirty-three days. Ken is nearby, David and Sylvia are there, Jennifer and Karen, Eva, Hans, the Scottish couple with the push cart.

I am going to continue my Camino at home, and joine the Rite of Christian Initiation in Adults

The Cathedral of Saint James is different from both Burgos and León. Each has their own splendor and each was filled with a reverent audience, touring and moving in quiet reflection. The western entrance,in the Façade of the Obradoiro, which faces the Plaza de Obradoiro with it's large doors leading to the Pórtico da Gloria and statue of the Saint were closed due to renovation, and instead we entered through south doors in the Façade das Pratarías (silverware)

A student of architecture could say more about the construction and style, but the most obvious space features include the long nave and the perpendicular transept. It is across the transept that the largest censor, an incense burner is swung on holy days and special occasions. Beneath the altar, a narrow stairwell and hallway includes a kneeler in front of the tomb and silver reliquary of Saint James.

Once back in the nave, I sat in a crowded kneeler.

There was a Pilgrim Mass in the Cathedral. The mass was spoken in Spanish, English and German.

I think I have known all along what would happen here, but I've not said it out loud or written it down, but it is very clear. The Sister's beatitudes include:

Blessed are you, pilgrim, because you have discovered the authentic Camino begins when it is completed.

I am going to continue my Camino at home and join the Rite of Christian Initiation in Adults program at Sacred Heart. I listened and heard the music and the message. I'm going to ask your mom to be my sponsor. I hope she says yes, and I hope you three will join me on the continued Camino of faith. I sat at the end of the mass, and then, with a new purpose and destination, I walked outside.

The streets were filled with celebrating pilgrims, happy tourists, and busy shops. I overheard a tour guide tell a group of cruise ship tourists that pilgrims must hike at least one hundred kilometers to receive their compostela. The tourists shook their heads in amazement. Later in the streets, I overheard two tourists talking, still amazed that someone might walk a hundred kilometers. I wonder what they would think of me and my companions walking eight hundred or more.

David had organized a final dinner. There were fifteen of us, new and old, around the table. It was a symbolic meal. The table was big. Hugh from Canada was there, as were two brothers from Israel and a couple from East Germany. David, Sylvia, Beth, and Sarah were there with Sandra.

At dinner, I sat with Brett, who was with us in Burgos. It completed the circle to have him with us again. Our conversation moved quickly from topic to topic, and we had several points of interest in common. He had taken photos all along the way, and I'm eager to see them when he posts them on his return to New Zealand.

F.R. "Fritz" Nordengren

While it defies practical and physical logic, I am convinced we will meet again. As I think of New Zealand, I think of the other countries around the table, and we turn and pose for a group photo.

For most of the dinner guests, this was the end. The Camino was over. When we walked back to the plaza and stood in the moonlight, I looked over my shoulder at the stairs that lead on the Camino to Fisterra. The bagpiper was playing in the arch. Tomorrow is another day. Seven days more, three to Fisterra, one to Muxía, three back to Santiago. It is my loop to the end of the world.

Love,

Dad

DAY THIRTY-FOUR:

"Begin new each day"

Negreira, October 24

Dear Chase, Noah, and Cara,

Next door to the albergue is a coffeehouse where they serve *chocolate y churros*. A pastry served with thick hot chocolate. Down the narrow streets are shops of all kinds—clothing stores, jewelry stores, shoe stores, and restaurants. Down the hill from the albergue is the Cathedral de Santiago and the Plaza del Obradoiro, where pilgrims rest and celebrate their arrival. To the left as you face the cathedral is the Parador Hotel, and it is there where once again into the morning I walked with my backpack in search of the yellow arrow and the Way, down the stairs and out into the streets of Santiago.

Like every day, it began new, but this beginning was a bit bittersweet. I have left many mornings with pilgrim friends still sleeping or while they lingered over breakfast or coffee or took time to write or phone family and friends. And each time, I was confident we would see each other again down the Way. Last night was the end for many of us. And while we might be able to stay in touch, the reality of life, distance, and time is that we will probably never see each other again. As another indicator of change, I also noticed I've cinched my belt another notch tighter.

The walk through the city winds up and into the suburbs and then cuts down a residential driveway, through a backyard, and onto a familiar style of trail into the trees. It was a reasonable walk but filled with rain. Midmorning coffee was in a tiny bar café in Os Arcos at the bottom of a hill. Three pilgrims from South Korea were there, too, and as we shed our ponchos and rain gear, the owner insisted on moving a stool closer to his wood stove so I could sit and dry the lower half of my pants. When I was drier, I got up and offered the stool to another pilgrim, who took a turn and shared in the host's kindness. I'm sure we made a mess, and the pilgrims who followed continued to track in the rain and muck during the day.

We were accompanied by rain all the way to Negreira. Our turn down a muddy road through the woods led to an urban street where the albergue we sought was closed. It was only the second closed albergue of the trip, and I didn't know if they were closed for the end of the season or for financial reasons. There were three others in town, so it was not a real concern.

I haven't done a look back at the Camino. I haven't thought about what I wished I had done more of or done less of. But the restaurant does prompt me to think about what I have missed on this trip. On nearly every international trip I've been on, there was always a moment when I became overwhelmed with a sense what am I doing here? It's not a panic attack, and it usually is at the end of a long period without sleep. I can remember struggling to stay awake during a welcome dinner in Viet Nam, slowly walking back to my room ready of a good nights sleep and finding a small green gecko on the sheets. A classic, what am I doing here? moment. I've had the feeling in India, Venezuela, South Africa, and even on week long fishing trips — usually when the action was slow. And in talking with other people who travel, they have had similar experiences.

Sandra started and finished the day with me. We shared a quiet dinner at the end of the day, but neither of us was as talkative as at our other dinners. She had two days of walking before she took a bus back to Santiago and then a flight home to Munich. The albergue had a handful of guests. No one seemed eager to make new friends, perhaps because of the rain, perhaps because it is the end of the Camino.

The restaurant dinner was average for what we have enjoyed on the Camino. Earlier in the day, in the town of Ponte Maceira, there was a stylish-looking restaurant on the way just before crossing the bridge in town. I missed Hans and wished he were here to give us the restaurant review. Perhaps it would have been the place to stay and each lunch.

Today was day thirty-four of walking, but in many ways, it felt like the first day. It was a day of unknowns. The French paper detailing albergues lists seven stops between Santiago and Fisterra. Each day is a long hike. There are fewer pilgrims, and more importantly, I have said goodbye to nearly everyone I have met along the way. This is a walk filled with more solitude.

Love,

Dad

DAY THIRTY-FIVE:

"The story tells itself in silence"

Olverio, October 25

Dear Chase, Noah, and Cara,

There have been signs, notes, and tokens left for others along the Way. I have walked along the trail to find an arrow shaped from pine cones or rocks. I've found hearts outlined in stone and filled with berries, spray-painted notes of gratitude and encouragement, paper notes and prayers stuck on crosses and left in sign posts, and the ever-present rock towers built by many pilgrims one at a time or all at once by one pilgrim. It was hard to know if some signs had been left that day, that month, or years ago.

"Julie, keep on walking." If you are Julie, this probably means a lot, even if it was written for another Julie.

Yesterday's rain filled what looked like normally dry streams and had turned the rocky trails to mud. It made for a sloppy walk but also made it easy to identify the pilgrims ahead of me by the boot prints or tire marks from the bicycles. And if you missed a turn, it was easy to know because the boot prints you were following were no longer there.

At the bottom of a hill, just after the small running water drainage from a field across the trail, someone had scrawled a note for another pilgrim in the mud. I paused to read it. In neat block letters drawn with a small stick were the words *CAMINO HEART*.

It could only be from Sandra, leaving it to encourage me. I had no idea how far ahead of me she was. It will encourage others, too, as they cross the same spot on the trail.

The rain continued on and off for most of the day. Near the top of a hill, a farmer moved his cows out onto the roadway to take them to a new pasture just as the rain intensified. Down the hill and around a bend in the road, I followed the cows. I could see a lake in the distance: Encoro da Fervenza. At the bottom of the hill was a covered bus stop shelter, but at that point in the day, I was as wet as I was going to be. I pulled the hood of the poncho off my face and kept walking. I waited with another pilgrim—the first one I had seen all day—at a narrow bridge as the oncoming and same-way traffic alternated. Then we hiked across the river, swollen from the continued rain.

Olverio has two albergues and a third a little further down the road, but I'd had enough for the day, and I stopped at the first albergue I came to. A woman took my money and in between rain showers walked me to a nice dorm. It was the first one I'd seen with a dehumidifier.

The albergue is set up a bit like a traditional motel. The restaurant and bar, which also has a small grocery, is in one building and perpendicular to the sleeping rooms. They have both dorm and single room accommodations.

I changed out of my clothes. My shoes were soaked, my socks drenched, I was in shorts and a t-shirt that were damp, but the poncho had kept me and my pack dry. I sat in the restaurant and store, keeping one eye out the window looking for pilgrims and the other on my crush, Toñi Moreno, and her TV show.

As other pilgrims come in, they changed out of their day's clothes and emptied their packs. Most of them had had water soaked into their packs, and all their clothes were wet and drying on improvised clotheslines in the albergue.

Blessed are you, pilgrim, if you discover the Camino holds a lot of silence, and the silence of prayer, and the prayer of meeting God who is waiting for you.

The Camino holds a lot of silence—or rather a lack of man-made sound. My note in my journal to you three was, "The story tells itself in silence." Back when I was walking the long power day on the Meseta, I wrote you about the spaces between the notes, the silence. As I think about the letters I've written you, I described a lot of the noise, the contact with pilgrims and the things we say, but it's the silence between the letters and between the events—or between the notes—that tells the story.

In today's silence, I spent time considering my choice to join the church. I have as many questions, or more, than I did before I had heard the calling on this walk. While I know some about the faith from my experiences with each of you, and I know some of the ritual and sacraments, there is a difference between knowing what others do and learning for yourself. It's about who you are when you are alone.

My dad used to say, "Never believe your own press releases." I suppose today, he would say, "Never believe your own profile." The point is, we can be lots of things to lots of people, but when were alone, when we are in the silence, is when we can reveal who we are.

Today in the silence, I'm still comfortable and happy in my choices. I wish the same for each of you.

Love,

Dad

DAY THIRTY-SIX:

"It isn't over when it ends"

Fisterra, the end of the world, October 26

Dear Chase, Noah, and Cara,

On paper, Cee looked like a nice seaside town and an easy place to stop for the day.
This morning, I had made up my mind to stop and to put Fisterra, the end, off one more day. Going all the way to Fisterra meant a forty-kilometer day. Twenty-five miles. I knew I had time to walk back or take a bus part or all of the way in order to make my flight out of Santiago.

Cara, I was thinking about you and your horse as I hiked out of Olverio. As I walked down the road, across the bridge, and up the hill toward O Logoso, I was met by a horse in the middle of the road. On the other side of a fence was a very nice pasture. I guessed he belonged there, but horses often know what is best. There have been a few dogs who have wandered with me, and I was trying to take time to recognize their presence when they spent time with me. The Camino may be the Way of Saint James, but I'm convinced Saint Francis called shotgun, having done his own pilgrimage to Rome.

Just before the incline down into Cee, I came to a brightly painted bollard kilometer marker. On the opposite side of the trail was a stump that was a well-worn perch for pilgrims pausing to take in the view. I stopped, set my pack down, and looked out at the Atlantic Ocean and the land mass that came to a point at Fisterra in the distance.

This was it. Pilgrims had come to this spot and seen their first view of the ocean for over a thousand years, perhaps as much as four to five hundred years before Columbus. I wanted to stop and stay here to watch the clouds on the horizon, the changing blue hue of the water, to see it at sunset and under the light of the moon.

A few minutes later, a couple with an English accent paused at the bollard, and I offered them a Choco Prince cookie. They declined.

"What a view. Do you think we have three or four minutes we can look?" she asked.

He replied with a curt, "Yes, I suppose we do."

"Is that Fisterra?" she asked, pointing in the distance.

"No, we can't possibly see it from here."

"Oh," she replied.

Then they picked up their packs and continued on the trail. I didn't have a watch, but it felt like three minutes exactly.

Everyone walks their own Camino.

I picked up, wandered through Cee, stopped at a midday mass, then pressed on up the hill, climbing the rest of the way to Fisterra and finally down into the town.

The Camino followed a boardwalk along the beach. The sea air and warm afternoon sun provided a triumphant ending to a day, unlike the rainy ending with yesterday's torrential downpour.

I climbed the hill and came to an albergue. It had a great view of the ocean but not much else, so I asked if there were others in town.

"Yes, several."

In a way, this was good news but in another way not. I knew I was walking on through Muxía and back to Santiago, but I had yet to meet anyone on the Way who was continuing to Muxía. Most had already taken a bus or were taking the bus back to Santiago.

I had made many of them a promise, a leap of faith, that I would see them "down the road." The odds of finding them now were growing slim.

I did a loop through the town and circled back, bypassing the municipal albergue and climbing a hill (reminding myself again that my joking meaning for *camino* is a Spanish word meaning *up*), and entered an albergue. It was bright, open, and had a nice feel.

I checked in, received my stamp, and walked back to the dorm, greeted by Eva. She had arrived by bus and was staying a few days before heading back. I dropped my backpack at the foot of my bed and looked across the aisle at the green backpack with the white scallop shell and the yellow flower. I shouldn't have been surprised. It was Sandra's.

We walked to the lighthouse, on the way pairing up with Frank and Helen. Walking toward us was the young Canadian man who had told me the story while we were in Astorga about singing "Ave Maria" in an empty chapel; the two Israelis from dinner in Santiago; and Peter and Kath from Australia.

Sandra took a final photo of me for Flickr. In it, I'm kneeling at the base of a concrete bollard marking kilometer 0.0 with the lighthouse behind me. By the time the sun set that night, I had said goodbye to nearly everyone I had met along the Way and many whom I knew only by face or backpack.

There were a few more goodbyes. Karen and Jennifer were having dinner at a seafood restaurant near the harbor. With them were a handful of pilgrims. I recognized them all but didn't know their names.

A bit further on, Sandra waved at the Frenchman with the big hair who had danced with his headlamp to *Swan Lake* and his walking partner. They waved us over to join them. They were beginning dessert, and we were ordering dinner.

The Frenchman announced he was "officially a tourist, no more pilgrim."

His friend agreed, as did Sandra, saying she was heading back on the bus in the morning.

"I walk on," I said. "I leave in the morning for Muxía, then back to Santiago."

"By foot?"

"Yes."

The Frenchman raised his glass in a toast. "To the last pilgrim."

We went our separate ways. Back in the albergue, Centenie was logging onto a computer in the common area. I asked her if she was going to Muxía. She said she was still deciding.

The Camino was geographically over. Kilometer 0.0 and the end of the world. It isn't over when it ends. I had to return to Santiago the way I came: by foot. One hundred ten kilometers to go. A rebirth and reentry to life. A physical metaphor of the Christian belief.

Love,

Dad

DAY THIRTY-SEVEN:

"Always wave goodbye"

Muxía, October 26

Dear Chase, Noah, and Cara,

Today is Sunday. This morning, I walked with a group of pilgrims from the albergue as they made their way to the bus stop for their return to Santiago. What takes three days by foot, they will cover in around three hours. I walked with them as far as the bus stop. Eva and I had said goodbye in the albergue before we left; she was staying on in Fisterra another day or two.

As Sandra and the others waited for the bus, I continued on to an open bakery, where I bought a loaf of bread for my hike to Muxía. As I paid, I spied the chocolate croissants in the case, still warm from the oven. I bought two, put the bread in my pack, and walked back up the hill toward the route to Muxía. At the corner, I stopped and gave Sandra one of the chocolate croissants. It was my way of saying thank you and goodbye. Sandra and I had passed each other on the Camino beginning day one on the trail up the Pyrenees just beyond Saint Jean. She was my guardian angel. We had walked many of the same stages together, and we had been separated by kilometers and days during the thirty-seven mornings of the Camino. She defined the Camino Heart. And today, she was on her way back to join her husband and her son, and the three of them would share stories of their

Caminos.

Surprisingly, we both knew exactly what to say to each other, the words that could encapsulate the emotion of sharing the pilgrimage with each other and the dozens of other pilgrims with whom we broke bread and drank café, Kas Limon, *vino tinto,* and water.

"Buen Camino," she said.

"Buen Camino," I replied.

I walked up the hill. I know this won't come as a surprise to you kids, but I don't do goodbye very well. In *Kolby Rae*, the main character makes fun of Joshua, her lover, because he doesn't wave goodbye when her sister drives off for an out-of-town meeting. She tells the man, "You have to wave goodbye."

I guess I don't wave goodbye, either, but I took some of the advice from my character in my book. I stopped, turned. and waved goodbye to Sandra and the others. I was blessed to see the people I had walked with the most and say goodbye to my guardian angels and my Camino Hearts.

I walked to the beach, took off my hiking shoes and socks, and walked in the surf and sand, eating the chocolate croissant and listening to the morning. It must have been on a beach like this where Jesus first called to Simon and Andrew, and then to James and John, telling them he would make them fishers of men. It's a good thought for the day, and in true Sunday tradition, a chocolate pastry after the reading.

When the croissant was gone, I walked up the beach and stopped at the faucets to rinse off my feet. I was greeted by a dog, a lab, who stayed as I dried my feet, put my shoes on, and pulled the lacing snug. The dog looked as if he had seen too many pilgrims do this too many times. He lost interest and continued exploring the sand and the beach grass.

I climbed the hill, passing a small hotel, when above me I heard, "Buen Camino." Hugh, the Canadian, waved.

I waved back. "Are you going to Muxía?"

"We'll see" he said.

"Buen Camino."

And then I left the city at the end of the world.

There are many smells along the Camino. The wild fennel was something I first recognized the morning I met Peter and Kath on the hike up to Alto del Perdón walking out of Cizur Menor. Throughout the hike, it was a companion, a bit of assurance that I was headed the right way. I know from my own experiences at Two Mile Ranch that each season has its own smells. A pilgrimage in spring and in winter would smell different.

I waved to a pilgrim outside the San Martiño De Duio church as he was jotting in his notebook.

According to tradition, this is the community and church where the disciples of Saint James sought permission to bury his remains in Spain. It wasn't until hours later, at the corner in a tiny town, that I saw other pilgrims. I met a couple and a German shepherd. The dog was friendly and walked between us, first with the couple, then back with me.

After a kilometer, I asked if the dog was theirs.

"No," they replied, adding they thought the dog was mine. He walked with us for several kilometers before dashing into a farm field to play with another dog.

The couple walked faster than me, and due to distance and the hills and curves of the paths, I didn't see them again. I saw one other couple and no one else until the end of the day's walk.

Just outside of Muxía, I met the trio of South Koreans I had seen off and on since Sahagún. As we wound through town, I walked with a family of four to a contemporary-styled albergue. I was tired and knew I had the pilgrim-in-the-headlights look, but I drew a breath and waited as the family talked with the hospitalero. I didn't follow their conversation closely, but the family seemed agitated. The parents wanted a room, the teenagers were in the bunk beds, and there was some issue about the price.

The hospitalero looked at me, rolled his eyes, and then escorted them to their room and beds. He returned, and I asked for a room and to rent and a towel in the best Spanish I could muster. He gave me the tour, found me a fresh towel, and showed me the cappuccino machine and his favorite flavor.

In the common area of the albergue, with tables for dining and chairs for reading, I waited for my laundry to dry and struck up a conversation with another pilgrim. I listened to him talk about how awful his Camino had been and how the country of Spain needed quiet doorstops. "All night long, the doors, *bang bang bang*."

On my way to dinner, I met two women who were dining in. They were the opposite of the man. Sherrie and her friend had high spirits and were infectious, joyful souls, both filled with the spirit of the Camino. Their enthusiasm tempted me to stay another day in Muxía to watch the waves crash on the stones surrounding the Virgen de la Barca to sample the seafood and find some music.

But I have three more days ahead of me, walking opposite the route arrows. The stretch from Muxía to Hospital will be the most tricky. And this time of year, based on what I've read and what other more experienced pilgrims have told me, I don't expect to see many others walking back from or walking ahead to Muxía.

There is no deadline, no rush. True, I have air reservations out of the country in four days and only three days of walking ahead of me. I have options: a taxi or a bus for any or all of the journey. But I am committed to walking, and I want to bank the extra day in case I wander too many kilometers off the Way and need to spend an extra day getting back.

They call the coast here Costa da Morte, "the coast of death," because of the many shipwrecks throughout history. After the celebrations in Santiago and Fisterra, today's walk alone, the rain, and the Sunday quiet felt very much like a funeral. As I write that, I remember that there was a funeral outside the albergue this afternoon. The metaphor continues.

Tomorrow is a new day.

Love,

Dad

DAY THIRTY-EIGHT:

"Turn around to see where you've been to know where you're going"

O Logoso, October 27

Dear Chase, Noah, and Cara,

The Camino is well marked. The yellow arrows show the way all the time. The road to Fisterra is well marked, too, as is the road to Muxía. On this latter section of the Way after Santiago, the arrows are double ended and labeled with an *M* or *F* for Muxía or Fisterra.

There are fewer people on this part of the Camino, even during the busy season. I saw only a handful of people on yesterday's Fisterra–Muxía path. I anticipated walking alone most of the way back to Santiago.

I was right. I saw no pilgrims between Muxía this morning and O Logoso, my stop for tonight. It was a long hike. O Logoso is the town where Cara's surrogate horse greeted me two days ago.

The time alone was a gift. The marking was adequate—for pilgrims walking from Santiago to Muxía. Going the reverse direction, the arrows are on the opposite side of signs or trees or buildings. That wasn't too bad. After thirty-seven days, one begins to get a sense of where arrow painters might think to paint an arrow. The real challenge came at crossroads.

I wandered off the Way twice today. Not far, but I wandered in a circle for a kilometer or more both times. The best solution in each case was to find the most recent marker, turn around, and try to see which path made the most sense. Sometimes to see where you're going, you have to stop and see where you've been.

As I walked, the lyrics of "Me and Bobby McGee" started in my head and then became full voice as I rounded the bend in the trail. Janis sang the hit, but I remember that Roger Miller sang an earlier version.

Thinking about Miller, I changed songs, and next I was singing "King of the Road." The second time through, I paused on the line about no phone, pool, or pets. I chuckled, realizing I'm not the first solo walker to think of this line. In Jon Krakauer's book *Into the Wild*, he quotes Chris McCandless's words, "Two years he walks the earth. No phone, no pool, no pets, no cigarettes. Ultimate freedom. An extremist. An aesthetic voyager whose home is the road."

That phrase caught my curiosity. Ultimate freedom. Kevin, in real life, back in Zubiri told me he planned to "walk the world."

I think about McCandless and then "King of the Road," which brings me back to Roger Miller, then to "Me and Bobby McGee."

I sing the line, "Freedom's just another word for nothin' left to lose."

After thirty-eight days walking the road, I have a fuller understanding of McCandless, and Jules, and Kevin. And Genesis 13:17: "Get up and walk through the land, across its length and breadth, for I give it to you." There is something very innate and natural about walking. Distance walking is not at all like walking a block to a parking space or around the park with the dogs.

The highlight of today was reaching the Hospital corner, a three-way intersection that divides the path from Santiago to Fisterra or Muxía. From here, my path heads east. It's a path I traveled before while heading west to Fisterra. Even in reverse, it was familiar.

I pressed on until I reached O Logoso and stopped for today. The big family with the rolling cart had taken over the top floor of the albergue. They deserved it. The older kids were watching Spanish TV. At the bar, I met a Spanish man who was hiking from Santiago to Fisterra. He had a sample of Camino life and now wanted to walk the entire route. Our dinner table had four pilgrims. We talked and laughed until the owners brought us a nightcap and we went to bed.

In my notebook, I tallied the distances remaining: 3 + 32 + 21 kilometers with the note "only 56?!" In looking at this, I don't know if that is an exclamation because fifty-six is a long distance or a short distance. But the number is fifty-six kilometers (thirty-five miles) to walk.

Love,

Dad

DAY THIRTY-NINE:

"Stop short of your goal if it helps your chance of success"
Vilaserío, October 28

Dear Chase, Noah and Cara,

As I left the albergue in O Logoso, I shouldered my pack and headed east. I had gone about fifty meters when the owner yelled from the door, "Santiago *o* Finisterre?"
"Santiago," I replied and pointed east.
"Santiago?" he questioned.
"Si."
"Buen Camino."
It might have been easy to go the wrong way. David, on the hill outside of Astorga, rang his bell if a pilgrim walked east instead of west. This hospitalero, with a watchful eye, made it a point to call out to me. Just over the crest of the hill, I came to the pasture where I had met Cara's surrogate horse on the way to Fisterra. This morning, he was in the pasture, eating and enjoying the morning light. Forgive me for talking to him, but I thanked him for suggesting I stop at O Logoso. I've been on the road for nearly forty days. I'm entitled, I think, to some quirkiness.

There were fifty-six-odd kilometers to go in reverse but over a familiar road. It was two days of nice walking, but the decision and challenge was the location of the albergues. There were three to choose from, one each in the towns of Santa Marina, Vilaserío, Negreira.

Fifty-six kilometers is a bit over thirty-four miles. A bit of a stretch for one day, although I've done two days over thirty miles early in the hike. I chose to walk a long stretch today to Negreira, staying in an albergue recommended at the table the last night by two women from Germany.

I hiked along and missed a turn. I went a kilometer or two down the highway before I realized I hadn't seen a way marker. I turned around and found one. I did the same thing again, clearly off the Camino, walking down a highway. I had no idea where I was.

It's not really possible to be lost on the Camino, though. There are towns with phones and businesses and restaurants and bars and hundreds of helpful people. About the only way to be lost would be to take off into the woods away from any road or trail. Nevertheless, you can spend hours being someplace that isn't really where you had in mind. It happened a third time today, too.

Even though I had only two more days to walk, I decided to buy a new set of replacement insoles for my shoes. I asked the pharmacist how to get back to the Camino. He gave me directions that included walking four kilometers down the road I was headed before turning left.

I think they were good directions, but going another four kilometers made me think how much farther I could be from where I wanted to go. I thanked the pharmacist and continued down the street, looking for another place to ask for directions.

I walked into a combination coffeeshop and store and asked for directions to the Camino. The clerk said to go back to the supermercado (I had seen two), turn right, and go about a kilometer. That sounded more reasonable—at least it had a shorter distance to be off track if wrong.

I turned at the supermercado and walked—first one kilometer, then another—and still saw no sign of the Camino. I crested a hill and saw a small trail off to my right. But there were no marking signs or clues this trail was the Camino. I asked Saint James for a sign. Saint James had not abandoned me on this trip, and he has protected pilgrims for centuries. This was a good time for him to give me a sign.

In front of me was a fork in the road. The road ahead continued straight and then curved right out of sight. My view of the road to the left was obscured by a large sign. Something moved and caught my eye. At first, I thought it was a tarp stuck to the base of the sign. I looked again. It was a pilgrim standing in his poncho.

Trying to conceal my excitement and relief, I blurted, "Do you speak English?"

"Yes."

"Which way to Santiago?"

He pointed straight down the road toward the curve.

"Thank you."

Once beyond the sign, I looked over my shoulder and remembered the turn and the sign. I looked further and recognized the lake, Encoro da Fervenza, in the distance. I remembered this place from day thirty-five on the way into Olverio.

I walked on to Vilaserío and stopped in the bar to find out where to check in at the albergue. It was time to stop for the day. I had a long day ahead tomorrow, and today I had walked extra hours trying to find my way.

I was alone there until three pilgrims joined me before sunset. Oddly, the albergue began to fill after dark and was full by the time I fell asleep. I can guess that they had hiked from Santiago in one day, ending their own long days on their way to Fisterra or Muxía

This morning, my plans were to walk all the way to Negreira, leaving a short morning walk into Santiago as I had done at Monte do Gozo the night before arriving in Santiago the first time. But tired, hungry, and ready for rest, I stopped short today.

After wandering as far off the Way as I had, I don't know what distance I covered. My notes say thirty-four kilometers from Vilaserío to Santiago. Roughly six and a half hours of walking tomorrow, and I'll be done with my journey of one thousand kilometers in forty days.

Love,

Dad

DAY FORTY:

"Arrive with others"

Santiago de Compostela, October 30

Dear Chase, Noah, and Cara,

Blessed are you, pilgrim, if what concerns you most is not to arrive, as to arrive with others.

This is the thought I woke with in Vilaserío this morning, my final morning of the Camino. I gathered my sleeping bag and my pack and walked down the stairs to put on my shoes. Out the door, up the stairs, and down the road, looking over my shoulder at the yellow arrows pointing the way behind me to Fisterra. Breakfast and café solo was twelve kilometers down the road in Negreira. I was there in a couple of hours.

Even walking in reverse, retracing the steps I had made six days ago, the route was familiar. The power of visual memory is amazing to me. I walked past the inviting and upscale restaurant in Ponte Maceira again but decided I clearly wasn't dressed for lunch. As well, I still had food in my pack. By the middle of the afternoon, I was walking through the eucalyptus woods along the Way.

I snacked on the food, and as I finished each piece, I said thank you to the folks who had suggested the snacks to me. I finished the Choco Prince cookies (thanks, Sandra), and I finished the Corn Nuts (thanks, Beth) as I got closer to Santiago. The last snack in my bag was a bag of olives (thanks, Maria). I finished those climbing a hill, both grateful for the shade and aware that soon the shade was going to end and I'd be walking into the city in the afternoon sun.

On day thirty-two, when we were at Monte do Gozo and we could see the cathedral at Santiago, many pilgrims became emotional. I was happy to see it, but to be honest, I didn't feel an emotional connection. Even in the square on day thirty-three, I loved the feeling of success, but the sight of the cathedral did not impress me much that day.

As I climbed the hill today and walked out of the eucalyptus trees, the path crossed someone's backyard and continued up their driveway and into the street. From there, I saw the returning pilgrim's first view of the cathedral.

I felt the breath leave my body. My eyes filled with tears of gratitude. I gave a broad smile and let out a yell. I had done it. I had walked to the end of the world and back. I had seen the metaphor of my life from birth to death and was now on my way back to Santiago and a final Pilgrim's Mass. The feeling was freeing. A spiritual rebirth.

I returned to Buen Camino's recommended albergue next to the bakery with the awesome chocolate y churros and close to the narrow shopping streets and the cathedral. I checked in and met the bunkmate on the diagonal bunk. He was Australian and had been touring the city. We swapped a few stories, and he headed out for more sightseeing.

After a shower, I walked around Santiago, looking in shop windows, watching both tourists and pilgrims ending their journey. As I was standing in front of a display of leather goods, I heard a woman call my name.

I turned. It was Lisa from day nine and the ghost town of Cirueña. She was standing with my Australian bunkmate from the albergue. It turns out they are brother and sister. The three of us had dinner of tapas, finished a bottle of wine, and then said our goodbyes. She was my final pilgrim goodbye.

The Sisters of the Sacred Heart wrote about arriving with others. I joked that I had walked the Camino with a hundred thousand of my closest friends, and the group of people I carry in my Camino Heart are more than one hundred thousand strong in spirit even if fewer than a hundred in body.

I stopped in the cathedral for a prayer. I prayed the longest list of names from my friends met along the way. It was here that I made my decision to begin RCIA. My prayer began with each of you and then Lisa; her brother; Sandra; Hans; David; Sylvia; Beth and Sarah; Eva; Frank; Helen; Scotland Ken and Australia David; Buen Camino; the Canadian singer; the Israeli brothers; the young tai chi couple so eager to learn; the Frenchman with big hair and his friend; Denmark and Papa Denmark; Jennifer; Karen; Brett; Centenie; Ralph; Bernard; Jacques; Ivan; Sherrie; the pushcart family; the pushcart couple; Alice; Bitte; Peter, John, and John and their wives; Lotus; Maria; Dan; the Boston family; Dave; Pam; Isabelle; Maxim; the forty hospitaleros; and the countless café owners.

While I set out on a journey of faith, I didn't know what that meant at the time, as with Martin Buber's quotation, "All journeys have secret destinations of which the traveler is unaware."

After forty days of walking and finding a lesson for each of you in every day, there are three things I heard that I want to share with you again. This is what the Camino taught me:

In Zabaldika, the sister of the Sacred Heart told me, "You must turn right and go to the church. It's up a hill, but you have to go uphill anyway."

In Carrión de los Condes, the pilgrim on his way to Rome stood in the church and spoke the only English I heard him say: "Buen Camino, I love you."

And David in front of his cantina cart just outside of Astorga told me, "Have a good life."

I love the three of you more than I can ever express. Every step is a gift.

Love,

Dad

F.R. "Fritz" Nordengren

About the Author

Who am I? Good question. Like you, I'm a lot of things to a lot of different people, but I am the resident writer at Two Mile Ranch, which is also home to the Iowa Writer's Retreat. I've been fortunate to publish two novels. I've also written articles and papers in my former job as a university professor. I've traveled a bit, and yes, I've had my share of life's ups and downs.

Even living on a quiet, rural retreat in a rustic cabin by two ponds, I knew it was time for a retreat of my own. I looked at many alternatives. One was a thirty-day silent retreat hiking the Appalachian Trail or the Pacific Coast Trail. I thought about biking across Iowa.

In the category of "You almost did what?," I was a finalist, but not selected, for a simulated mission to Mars conducted on the coast of Hawaii, helping researchers learn about food, taste, and menu fatigue. Yes, it was time for a retreat, but I had not found the right one.

I had heard of pilgrimages, and specifically the Camino, but knew very little about it. Shirley MacLaine wrote about it. Pope John Paul II dressed as a pilgrim on the hill outside Santiago for World Youth Day in 1989.

I was reminded of the Way when I watched Emilio Estevez's film of the same name. The movie, a buddy road trip story about a father mourning the loss of his son, follows four travelers on the Camino. I think it was the introduction of the Camino to many Americans. When I finished the film, I stepped out onto the deck that divides the dogtrot cabin at Two Mile and listened to the sounds in the sunset. In the moment of stillness, I knew I had to go. I had found my retreat. It called to me. As a colleague later said to me, "When you hear the Holy Spirit, you know."

There is a line in the trailer of the film where the father, played by Martin Sheen, tells the son, played by Estevez, "Most people don't have the luxury of just leaving it all behind." I'm not sure you leave it all behind on the Camino; rather, you focus on what is innate and essential. Your life continues. You wake, eat, walk, meet, and learn every day. Your friend's lives, your family's lives, your coworker's lives all continue. Nothing and no one is left behind.

In this modern world, however, traveling across the world for eight weeks does take planning and preparation. For me, that preparation took over a year. I had animals and livestock on the farm to finish growing out, to move, and to make arrangements for their care. I had to find the best time in both my writing and my teaching schedule to be away for two months. My decision to walk the Way and my departure were nearly fourteen months apart. In contrast, on the fourth day of my walk, I met a young Canadian. His preparation was a bit shorter: he learned about the Camino on a Monday, went to the sporting goods store to buy a pack and gear on Tuesday, and was on a transatlantic flight on Wednesday.

In short, this is two stories. In my forty days of walking, I sought each day to learn something, to find meaning in what I experienced, and to find experience in the meaning. The result is these letters to my children, one for each day of my walk. The second story is of my decision to become an adult candidate in the Catholic faith.

Before I left, the most common question I heard about my decision was, "Why are you doing this?" When I returned, the most common question was, "What was it like?"

To be honest, sharing these letters in this book is an answer to those questions. When I left, I was not Catholic, fifty-three years old, distant from each of my children, and separated from my wife. I was carrying weight that cannot be measured on a scale. My pack was twenty pounds; my burden was much more.

F.R. "Fritz" Nordengren

Made in the USA
Lexington, KY
08 April 2015